The West Coast Trail and Nitinat Lakes

The West Coast Trail and Nitinat Lakes

A Trail Guide by the Sierra Club of British Columbia

J. J. Douglas Ltd., Vancouver

ISBN   0-88894-018-1

J.J. Douglas Ltd.
3645 McKechnie Drive
West Vancouver, British Columbia

Typeset by Vancouver Freelance Litho-prep Ltd.
Printed and bound by Brock Webber Printing Co. Ltd.
Vancouver, British Columbia, Canada.

*This book is dedicated to those who,
through the years, have loved this land
enough to fight to preserve its
natural beauty for future generations.*

Acknowledgement

This book has been a co-operative effort of members of the Sierra Club of British Columbia who love the West Coast Trail and the Nitinat. To Humphrey Davy, Jim Hamilton and Hugh Murray we are indebted for their knowledge of the West Coast Trail and their pioneer efforts to secure park status for it.

The Victoria group of the Sierra Club have been the pioneers of the Nitinat Lakes, they made the early explorations, marked the trails and laboured on the portages. The dedicated efforts of Karen McNaught, Ric Careless, John Willow, Gordy Price, and their supporters, have given us all an inspired example.

This book was conceived by Sierra members in:
    Text – John Twigg and Ken Farquharson
    Illustration – Terry Schneider
    Photographs – Steve Cooke, Dean Goodman and
                 John Temple
    Maps – Jerry White and Peter Gose

Mouth of Hitchie Creek.

Contents

Rocks and cliffs, Tsuquadra area.

Introduction

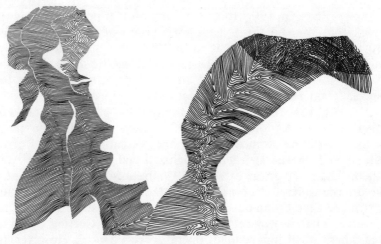

People never seem to be "just interested" in the 50 mile long West Coast Trail on the southwest coast of Vancouver Island. Either they are passionately involved with it, or barely aware of its existence. In recent years the number of people seriously interested in the trail has grown from a handful of wilderness buffs to thousands of Canadians who want to preserve its immense recreational value, and increasing numbers are actually hiking all or part of the trail.

In 1971 more than 2,000 people hiked the entire trail between Port Renfrew and Bamfield and many more spent a day or two exploring portions of it. Most of them became convinced that it should be set aside forever as a park: such is its beauty.

It is this group of people, those who have experienced the trail and its ability to spiritually rejuvenate people, that is one of the main forces in the current political controversy surrounding the trail.

The trail became a political football, of all ignominious things to become, in the summer of 1970 when it was included in Pacific Rim National Park. But the trail and the rugged coastline between Port Renfrew and Bamfield has been in the news since 1890. This portion of British Columbia's coastline has been the final resting place of about 60 ships since 1854, the latest being the wreck in the spring of 1972 when the freighter M.V. Vanlene spilled oil on the beaches of Cape Beale at the northern end of the trail.

In fact, the area became known as the "Graveyard of the Pacific" because so many ships drifted with the currents around Cape Flattery and slammed into the cruel shelf. The area was also

1

a graveyard for many people. Indians have been living and fighting on the coast since well before the first white men sailed past the island, and many people lost their lives in shipwrecks along the rugged coastline. The wreck of the S.S. Valancia just north of the Klanawa River in 1906 took the lives of 126 people. It was this wreck that spurred the federal government of that time into improving the rugged trail that until 1909 was little more than an animal path following a telephone wire along the shore. Remnants of the 1909 Life Saving Trail are what present day hikers use, especially on the northern parts of the trail.

Apart from the shipwrecks, the trail has been in the news for other reasons. As long ago as 1926, when the land resource in British Columbia seemed infinite, the recreation potential of the Nitinat and coastal area was recognized and a park reserve established. The reserve was lifted in 1947 because the government of the time considered the area too remote to be usable for recreation. A struggle then broke out within the forest industry for control of the area. First it was set up as the Clayoquot Cutting Circle, an area where small independent operators could work. However, the major companies had designs on the area and in 1957 the Clayoquot Circle was disbanded and the area put into Tree Farm Licences 21 and 27 managed by MacMillan Bloedel and British Columbia Forest Products. It was for accepting a bribe on the award of Tree Farm Licences in this period that the Minister of Lands and Forests was later convicted.

However, the Nitinat and the West Coast were still remote, and the timber on the land very old, much of it past its prime, so the forest companies did not begin to penetrate the area until after 1965, having exhausted their more profitable areas.

By this time hikers had become aware of the beauty of the area and were using the old trail despite its dilapidated state. They were helped by the Provincial Parks Branch which cleared and marked some of the worst sections at the south end.

While the trail was being used by growing numbers, the federal government was pressing the provincial government to include the trail and a few adjacent river basins in the Pacific Rim National Park. Their efforts bore fruit and when this park was created in April 1970, it included three portions: Long Beach, Effingham Islands and the West Coast Trail, between Port Renfrew and Pachena Bay, but the boundaries of the trail portion were left to be decided at some time before April 1974. The provincial government has taken the side of the forest industry and has been a reluctant partner in the discussion on the trail boundaries and is attempting to keep the boundaries as narrow as possible. Meanwhile the forest companies have been conducting a press release campaign against any enlargments to the proposed narrow boundaries for the West Coast Trail.

Which brings us back to the hikers whose very lives are threatened as a consequence of political considerations that place monetary values ahead of human and esthetic values. Why threatened? At present the trail is dangerous in several places (particularly where slippery logs are used to cross raging creeks) and some hikers will be killed or maimed unless the unnecessary hazards are removed. And the short-sighted policies of the provincial government may well mean that within 20 years the area set aside will be hopelessly inadequate as the trail becomes more popular.

The trail is still wilderness and hopefully it will be always. But "wilderness" park does not mean that it be left as an absolute raw wilderness. Raw wilderness on the west coast of Vancouver Island is like no other wilderness — it is strong enough to fight back and defeat human settlement. The town of Clo—oose for example, is now a ghost town and in a few years the buildings will be hidden by bush and knocked down by wind.

The area is extremely rough and hikers should be aware of what they will encounter. With proper preparations hiking can be enjoyed to the fullest, but with improper preparations can be a miserable experience. This book, in its handy, pack-pocket sized format, has been produced to help the hiker have an enjoyable trip. It includes advice on the kind of food to take and the clothes to wear. The maps contain the observations and suggestions of hikers who have been using the trail since it was first opened, so that you can benefit from their experience, so you will avoid attempting to cross the sea chasm north of the Walbran River when the tide is higher than six feet, and be aware of the dangerous winds of Nitinat Lake.

From all those who have contributed to this guide, good luck with the weather and enjoy your hike!

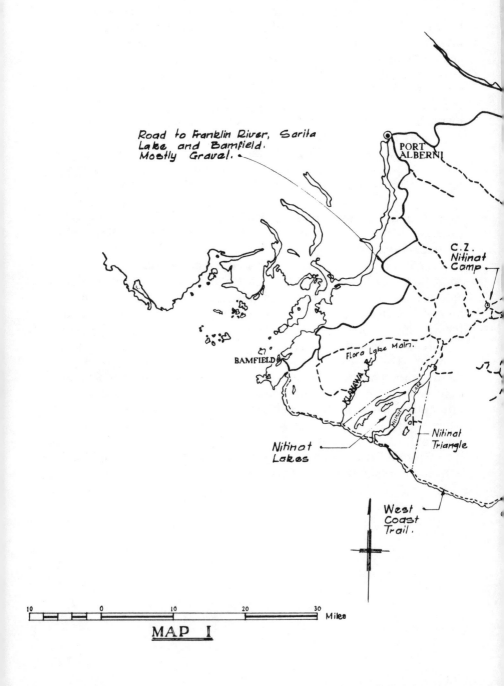

Road to Franklin River, Sarita
Lake and Bamfield.
Mostly Gravel.

PORT
ALBERNI

C.Z.
Nitinat
Camp

Flora Lake Main.

BAMFIELD

KLANAWA

Nitinat

Nitinat
Lakes

Nitinat
Triangle

West
Coast
Trail.

10   0   10   20   30   Miles

MAP I

See following companies for maps of logging roads.
Nanaimo Lakes - Crown Zellerbach
Port Alberni - Nitinat - MacMillan Bloedel
Lake Cowichan - Nitinat - B.C. Forest Prod.
Port Renfrew - B.C. Forest Products

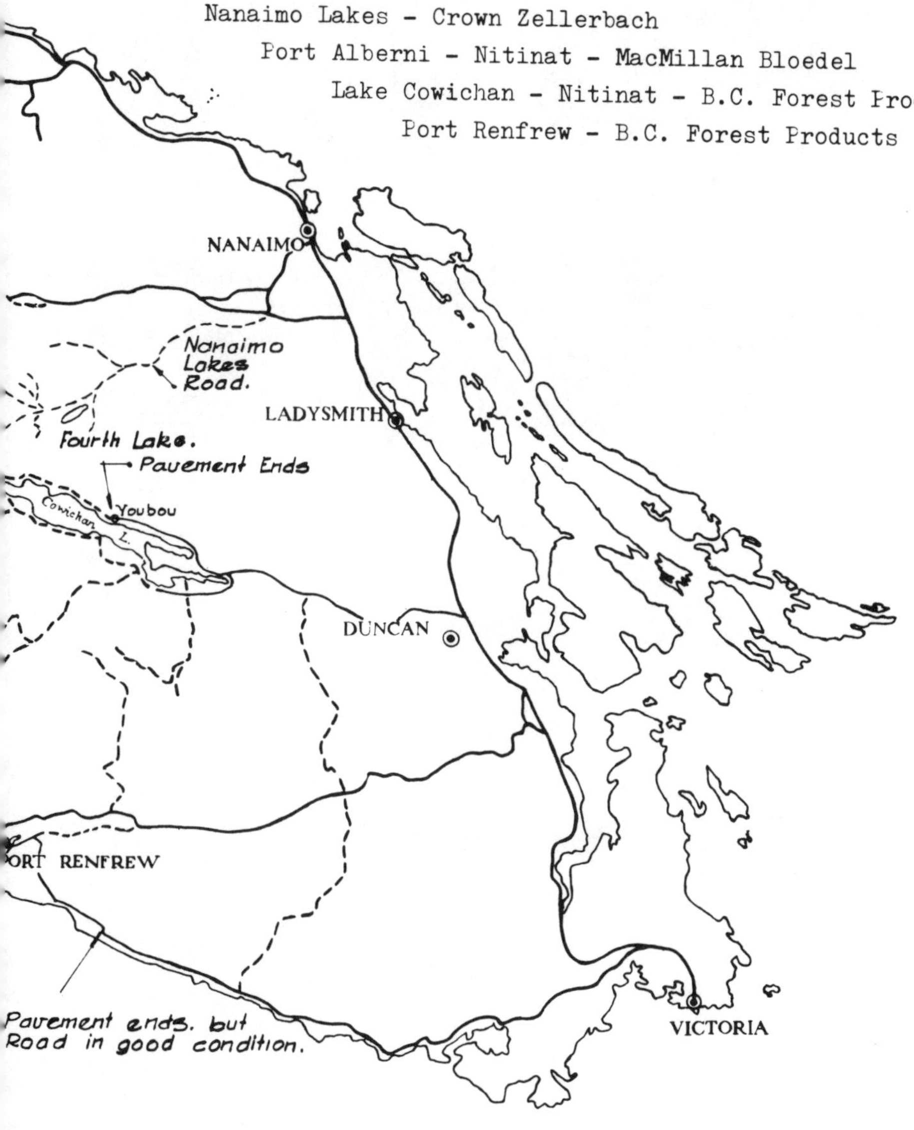

NANAIMO

Nanaimo
Lakes
Road.

LADYSMITH

Fourth Lake.
Pavement Ends

Cowichan L.   Youbou

DUNCAN

PORT RENFREW

Pavement ends. but
Road in good condition.

VICTORIA

1

On the beach near Nitinat Narrows.

The West Coast Trail

There are two methods of attacking the first section of the trail. You can start early in the morning and attempt to slog through to the cabin at Camper Bay by sunset or you can start later in the day and take the difficult portion between the Gordon River and Camper Bay in two steps. The method you choose should depend on the weather and such things as what time you arrive in Port Renfrew and cross the Gordon River. If the weather is wet, very few hikers are able to make it from the Gordon all the way to Camper Bay in one day. The first section of the trail is very difficult because there has been relatively little maintenance done on this section of the trail.

Much of the hiking in the first section is slogging up muddy stream beds and ducking or crawling under deadfalls. If your pack is heavy (about 40-50 pounds) and you just left the office the night before, it is probably best to take this section in two stages.

Crossing the Gordon River is accomplished by asking the people living on the Port Renfrew side of the Gordon River, who will take you to the tidal marker on the other side of the river for a fee of $2.00. Follow the trail since the beach is impassable. After about one and a half hours you will come across a donkey engine (4) left by loggers earlier in the century. Note that the forest around the southern portion of the trail is second growth, which accounts for the dense underbrush not found in other parts of the trail.

There is usually plenty of water from the many small streams along this hilly first section, so there is no need to carry full water bottles at this point. After about two hours of hiking through dense bush, the trail comes into an open area which gives excellent views of the bay and Port Renfrew across the water.

The first campsite encountered is also the highest point on the trail. The site is about 15 feet off the main trail, which follows a huge log and an old logging cable. There is plenty of good firewood left over from the logging operations and there is room for at least four tents. However, the nearest water is at (8), which is reached by a steep and difficult path. If your party does not need large amounts of water, it might be a good idea to fill up water bottles at one of the streams after the logging donkey. The campsite at (7) gives a beautiful veiw of the ocean and the distant Olympic Peninsula in Washington. The sunrise is particularly beautiful as it dissipates the heavy mists at the lower levels of the mountain.

The log crossing at (8) is a sample of things to come. If you bother to look down, you will see that the drop is about 30 feet into a raging creek. It's best not to look down and calmly trust your new Vibram soles.

The trail after the campsite is steep and scenically boring except for the beauty of the forest floor vegetation. The detour to Thrasher Cove is difficult but Thrasher Cove is beautiful and an excellent place to camp overnight. Once you reach the trail intersection at (13), the worst is over for a while. From there it is fast downhill hiking to 150 Yard Creek (16), so named because it is close to the ocean. The campsite here is small and extremely wet because it is in a gulley but it is a useful place to camp if you don't have enough time to make it to Camper Bay.

A few minutes out of the 150 Yard campsite is a side trail that leads to the beach. If the tide is out, it is worth the trouble to get down to the shelf because of the speed that can be made on the sidewalk-like beach. However, make sure the tide will stay out long enough to allow you to reach the next point that leads back up the cliff to the trail (20, 23).

The trail between (18) and (26) is often boggy since all the run-off from the mountains collects here. About now you will be looking forward to the dry socks in your pack.

One of the big myths that has developed about the West Coast Trail is the difficulty of the blowdown area (27). With good boots the blowdown area is actually a reprieve from the constant slogging in the first part of the trail. The blowdown is an area about the size of a city block containing trees fallen on top of each other. To cross the area one simply climbs up on top of the logs and walks along them. The logs are only 10 or 15 feet above the ground and the bark provides good traction. However, one should be careful to watch where the route goes and not take logs that lead to dead ends such as a narrowing log or one that ends in mid-air.

Incidentally, such blowdown areas will become more common if the provincial government permits logging companies to operate within one mile of the shoreline. The trees protect each other from such blowdowns by growing evenly so that the strong ocean winds pass overhead instead of swirling into open spaces. A good example of the forest protecting itself from ocean winds can be seen from the tidal marker at the beginning of the trail. If you look at the forest growing at the end of Port San Juan, you will see that it forms a remarkable wedge. Salal grows right down to the beach and all the way back to the first trees, forming a protective belt.

The trail from the blowdown area to Camper Bay is steep and usually muddy. There are no ropes to help you down the cliff, so just squat down and sort of slide. So what if you get muddy, the cabin is only minutes away. Crossing the creek is only dangerous if you lose your balance. However, there is little danger of being swept out to sea since the creek forms a shallow, slow-flowing pool in front of the cabin.

There are many techniques for creek crossing. One is, take off your boots and pants, cut a stave (remember that live trees have feelings too) and wade in. But the water is cold and the rocks are often slippery, so many hikers take their socks and pants off before putting their boots back on. Others bring a pair of light sneakers expressly for crossing such streams.

And then there are those who say, "What the heck!" and wade in fully clothed. They are also the ones who spend all night in the cabin trying to dry out their clothes.

The cabin at Camper Bay is a remnant of the days when the trail was maintained by linemen who lived in cabins placed at points along the trail. The cabin is falling apart now but the roof should be good for a few more summers. There are two bed-frames in the cabin and a small stove improvised from rusting metal. The smoke goes out the roof and so far it hasn't caught on fire. The windows, well, are partially filled with glass, plastic and nothing. It seems some people used the doors for firewood, so people have improvised doors out of the yards of plastic left by hikers.

The cabin is a welcome resting spot after the heavy going in the first section and if hikers are courteous (we all are, aren't we?), it should be treated respectfully.

The section of the trail between Camper Bay and Logan Creek is probably the most difficult section of the trail. No matter which path you choose, it involves wet and difficult hiking. Taking the trail involves climbing the log ladders behind the Camper Bay

9

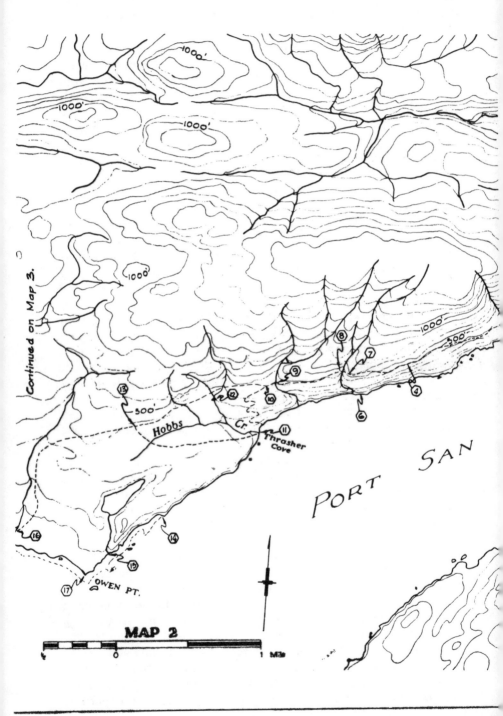

MAP 2

Continued on Map 3.

1000'
1000'
1000'
1000'
1000'
1000'
500'

⑧
⑦
⑨
④
⑬
②⑫
⑩
⑥
500'
Hobbs
Cr.
⑪
Thrasher
Cove

PORT   SAN

⑯
⑭
⑮
⑰ OWEN PT.

0   1 Mile

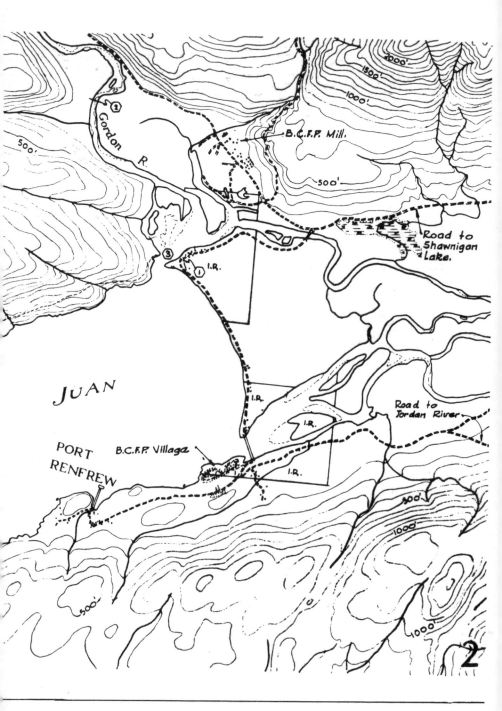

(1) Home of Chief Charley Jones. He will ferry you across the Gordon River, $2.00 per person.

(2) Bridge, under construction in 1972.

(3) Pink tidal markers, beginning of West Coast Trail.

(4) Donkey engine, as much as 2 hours' hike from the beginning of the trail.

(5) Impassable cliff.

(6) Steep gravel slope just below trail. Beach access in emergency. Beware of landslides.

(7) Highest point on trail, small campsite, water usually at (8). Between (6) and (7) trail passes through open area, with good views.

(8) Small stream crossed on log.

(9) Log Jam Creek, about 3 hours from Port Renfrew. Pleasant rest stop, possible campsite.

(10) Intersection of first Thrasher Cove Trail (20 mins. to cove). Trail is steep and poorly marked in open areas.

(11) Thrasher Cove. Excellent camping. Water at Hobb's Creek.

(12) Pretty falls, but difficult access.

(13) Intersection of second Thrasher Cove Trail (50 mins. to cove), 30 mins. from (9).

(14) Sandstone shelf begins.

(15) Cleft Falls.

(16) 150 Yard Creek. Good, small campsite, 45 minutes from (13). Interesting with pool and cavern below campsite.

(17) Owen Point. 50 mins. from (11). It is possible to walk around point if tide below 6 feet, a trail exists over point. Area to west known as 'Moonscape' because of unusual eroded sandstone.

(18) First beach access trail. 5 mins. from (16).

cabin and then slogging along dull trail until (28). However, at (28) there is an expansive view of the ocean. Some hikers report that the beach route to the creek at (33) is usable. If you try it, make sure you have enough hours of low tide to enable you to reach the trail access at (33).

The land route from (33) to Sandstone Creek is in poor condition, especially during wet weather. The beach route offers fast hiking but some difficulty regaining the trail via the creek bed. The trail is probably the safest route for inexperienced hikers.

Crossing the Cullite can be difficult if the river is high. There is a usable campsite on the Camper Bay side of the creek but the creek gulley is usually so wet that it is difficult to maintain a cooking fire. In such cases a small gas burner is worth its weight in a pack.

The trail from Cullite to Logan is wet but fast and interesting. The long bog is crossed on planks and small logs, or by slogging through the mudholes that are as much as 10 inches deep. However, the plant life in this bog is interesting because there is no forest cover and only short pine trees.

There is good camping on the Bamfield side of the Logan Creek beach. Under an average flow, the creek is not difficult to cross. It is easiest near the mouth, and if the logs are used, it is possible to avoid soaking your boots. Logan Creek is a good place to stop for lunch, wait for a low tide or spend the night. There is good beachcombing here because it is the most southerly beach along the trail that collects flotsam from the open ocean. Consequently, it is a good place to look for glass fishing bulbs from Japan.

The section from Logan Creek to the Carmanah area is dangerous because it requires crossing two deep creeks as well as tricky chasms if the beach route is followed. The trail route is dull but easy hiking along the now more level terrain. The beach route is fast and interesting but can be used only when the tide is below six feet and the seas are calm. The tide problem is at (45) where a deep sea chasm runs all the way to the cliff. The chasm can be crossed only if the waves are small and the tide is low enough to expose a rock in the middle of the chasm. The crossing is further complicated by a waterfall which falls directly onto the crossing and makes all the rocks slippery.

At Walbran there is a semi-permanent shelter on the beach as well as lots of open space for tents. There is plenty of firewood but the wind coming off the ocean at night is generally cold and moist.

Crossing the Walbran usually requires building a raft and return system well upstream. There is a cable on the Bamfield side of the creek that makes a good place to secure a rope. The shelf

13

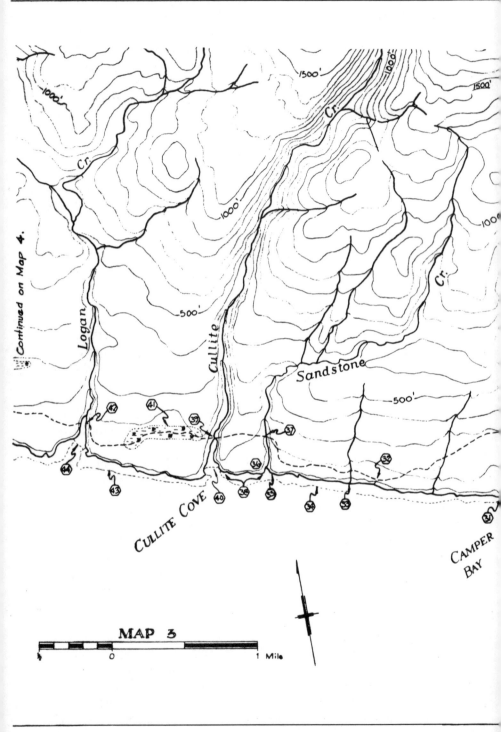

Continued on Map 4.

1500'

1000'

1500'

1000'

Cr.

Cr.

1000'

1000'

Cr.

1000'

Logan

Cullite

Sandstone

500'

500'

42

41

39

37

32

34

38

43

CULLITE COVE

40

36

35

34

33

31

CAMPER
BAY

MAP 3

0   1 Mile

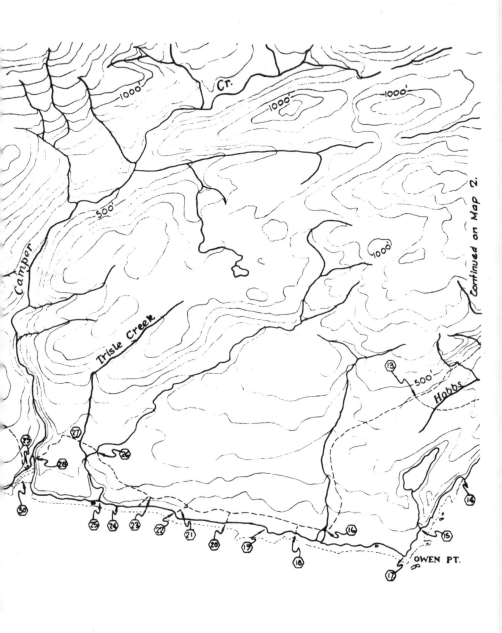

Cr.

1000'

1000'

1000'

1000'

500'

Camper

Trisle Creek

13

500'

Hobbs

Continued on Map 2.

27

26

22

29

30

25

24

23

22

21

20

19

18

16

14

15

17

OWEN PT.

3

(19)   Small shady cove 30 mins. from (17).

(20)   Second beach access trail, 15 mins. from (18).

(21)   Small trail to edge of cliff.

(22)   Small, shady cove.

(23)   Third (last) beach access trail, 25 mins. from (19).

(24)   Tidal pool area, rich marine life and swims.

(25)   Sandstone shelf ends in deep, wide, impassable channel, good camp-site at mouth of Trisle Creek.

(26)   Small campsite on creek, waterfall short way upstream.

(27)   Severe "Blowdown Area." Use extreme caution, and follow route marked out over logs.

(28)   Camper Creek. Impassable and very dangerous in high water.

(29)   Old cabin, good shelter in rain, but undesirable otherwise. Resumption of trail.

(30)   Camper Bay has excellent campsite where it is possible to land a boat in calm seas. Camp unreachable when creek is high.

(31)   Sandstone shelf broken by channel which is impassable at high tide. If this is passable then so will be the rest of the route to Sandstone Creek. A bypass trail has been cut over the break.

(32)   Short Trail to cliff's edge. Beautiful view.

(33)   Beach access from trail down this creek bed.

(34)   Seals often sighted here.

(35)   Sandstone shelf ends, access to trail up creek bed. Climb off shelf onto rocks and into ocean (will be thigh-deep at most, if (31) is passable). It is very hard to climb up onto this shelf, consequently hikers going towards Port Renfrew should take the trail.

(36)   To get back to the trail, cross over creek on log jam, and continue walking up to 15-foot waterfall. Cable to right of waterfall as you face it, allows you to pull yourself up bank. Trail crosses creek immediately upstream from waterfall.

(37)   Sandstone Creek. Good rest stop but no campsite. 2¼ hours from (29) by trail. Least dangerous of these creeks in high water.

(38)   This portion of sandstone shelf cannot be reached while carrying pack.

(39)   Cullite Creek. 20 mins. from (37). Impassable and very dangerous when high.

(40)   Cullite Cove. Beautiful campsite, unreachable when creek is high.

(41)   Swamp, no forest cover, possible helicopter landing. Very interesting botanically.

(42)   Logan Creek. 50 mins. from (40). Impassable and dangerous when high. Old cable from crossing still strung across creek. Gorge and potholes 1/2 mile upstream.

(43)   This shelf uninteresting.

can be waded at low tide but waders should be careful to keep their footing in the constantly-changing creek bed. Sending one person at a time, and tying a rope to him is a safe way to cross the shelf. Once across the Walbran, it is only a few hundred yards to a long sandy beach. Hiking from the Walbran to Carmanah looks easy because of the long sandy beaches, but the sand is so fine that it is like walking on sand dunes. In other words, you must learn a new style of hiking. After a while, you will be able to find where the sand is hardest. Good places to try are at the water's edge, at high tide marks, and in darker sand. When the tide is out, the shelf also provides good hiking.

The Carmanah is a very difficult creek to cross during high flows, when it is usually deep and fast. It is wise to use a stave and boots here. Shortly after the creek is the Carmanah lighthouse, which is first sighted at Bonilla Point. The lighthouse keepers are usually working or sleeping, so you should realize that these keepers see at least 2,000 hikers each summer, and not bother them with your experiences. They have probably heard many similar tales before. There are only emergency campsites on the beaches between Walbran and the lighthouse because the driftwood is pushed right to the bushes. Also, there are few good creeks along the long beaches, so if you have a tendency to get thirsty you should carry a small waterbottle.

The best campsite near Carmanah is a small red cabin on the logged-off point at (51), though there could be a problem obtaining firewood. After that is an excellent cabin with beds and a stove at (54). Either of these two cabins are good places to hike in one day from Walbran or Logan Creek. The drinking water problem can be solved by filling up water containers at a suitable creek shortly before choosing a campsite.

The next section of the trail, from the Carmanah area to Nitinat Narrows, is by far the most enjoyable part of the trail since there are many sights of geographical and historical interest. The only difficult part of the section is at (56) where a sea chasm blocks the shelf. A passable route has been built through the salal behind the tree, but it is easiest to rejoin the trail at (55) because the trail is in good condition.

The trail rejoins the beach at (57) where a bridge over a small creek has rotted and been washed out. The beach should be followed to the Lookout, a small cabin built between the beach and the large sand dunes that used to be a garden when Clo—oose was a thriving village earlier in the century. The two trails from the Lookout both end at the suspension bridge across the Cheewhat at (58). However, the route with the telephone wire is shorter. The other trail that leads north-easterly takes hikers to the remnants of

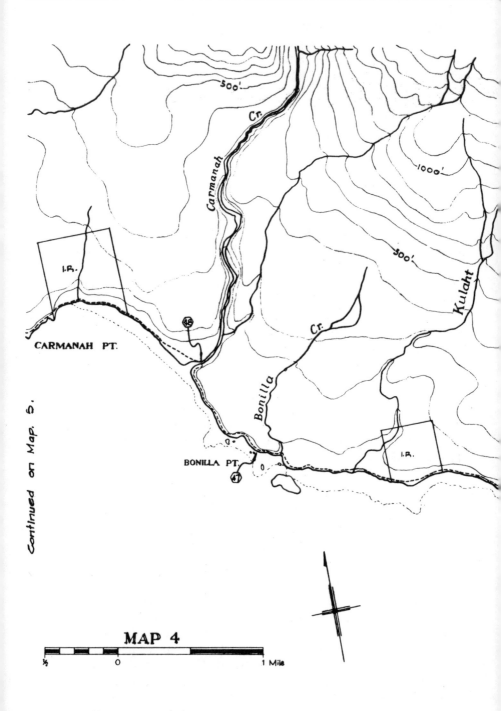

500'

Carmanah Cr.

1000'

500'

Kulaht

I.R.

Cr.

45

CARMANAH PT.

Bonilla

Continued on Map. 5.

BONILLA PT.

47

I.R.

MAP 4

½   O   1 Mile

18

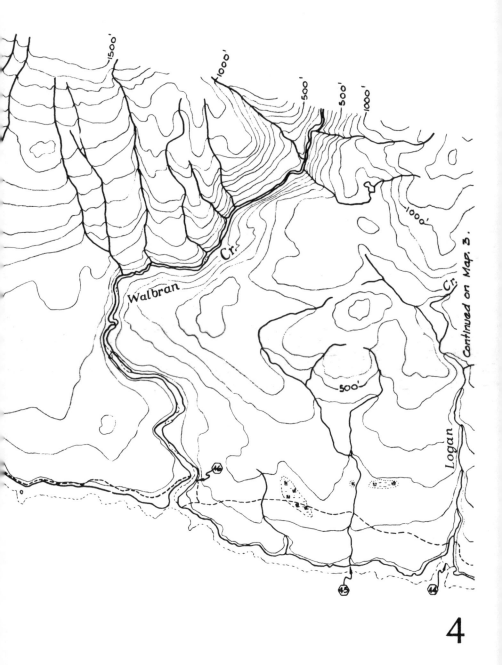

Walbran Cr.

Logan Cr.

Continued on Map. 3.

4

(44)   Good campsite on beach by creek, unreachable when creek is high. It is possible to walk from here to Clo–oose at low tide, but note *(40)*.

(45)   Waterfall and channel in sandstone shelf, very slippery. Passable only at low tide (below 5.5 feet), in dry weather and calm seas. Should be attempted only by parties of two or more with rope.

(46)   Walbran Creek. Trail between here and *(34)* is good 1¼ hours. Excellent campsite, good swimming. Creek is impassable and extremely dangerous when high. Walk from here to Carmanah Lighthouse by beach (passable at high tide, best at low).

(47)   Bonilla Point is marked by a huge triangular sign sticking out of the bush.

(48)   Carmanah Creek, impassable and extremely dangerous when high, 1¾ hours from *(46)*. Good campsite on lighthouse side of creek.

old houses. The houses were built in an area that is out of the ocean wind, and is thus very peaceful. If the weather is good there are probably good places to camp in the old gardens.

The Cheewhat is a deep, slow-flowing river called "River of Urine" by the local Indians. Better drinking water is available from the many small creeks in the Clo—oose and Cheewhat area. The suspension bridge across the Cheewhat is in excellent condition and a favorite subject of photographers. The board-walk path that begins on the Clo—oose side of the bridge should be used with caution since some of the boards are rotting. However, if you are careful to step on two boards or above the log supports, there is relatively little danger of falling through. A good technique for this and all boardwalks farther north is to walk on the side nearest to the ground unless the boards are slippery, in which case it might be wise to leave the boardwalk. If you place your foot half on one board and half on another, you still have half a chance of keeping your balance if the board breaks. Also, maintaining a medium speed allows you to keep going forward instead of down if a board breaks.

Clo—oose proper is an excellent place to stop and spend a few days poking around the many attics. A creek provides usable drinking water if it is taken upstream from all the garbage, and several cabins provide protection from rain. The cabins were used first by people who attempted to make Clo—oose a resort colony and in the late 1920's and early 1930's the village was a missionary town. The first settler in the area came about 1889 and a cabin containing a complete set of the 1888 Encyclopedia Britannica is still standing in the western part of Clo—oose.

The trail from Clo—oose to Nitinat Narrows follows the shoreline and takes about half an hour to walk. Be careful to take the trail marked "Nitinat Narrows". The other trails lead to Brown's Bay, which is an isolated boat moorage on Nitinat Lake. Clo—oose Lake on the Brown's Bay trail is a pretty lake and probably good for swimming.

At Whyac there are usually members of the Nitinat Indian Band who will take you across the dangerous narrows for a nominal fee, usually $2.00 per person. Both Whyac and Clo—oose are Indian Reserves and the land should be treated with respect. Whyac is a very old village, possibly one of the oldest on the West Coast of North America, its mystical atmosphere is one of the highlights of the hike. If there is no one in the village to take you across the narrows, you should wait rather than attempt to cross by yourself. The tide through the narrows is extremely rapid and has claimed many lives in the past.

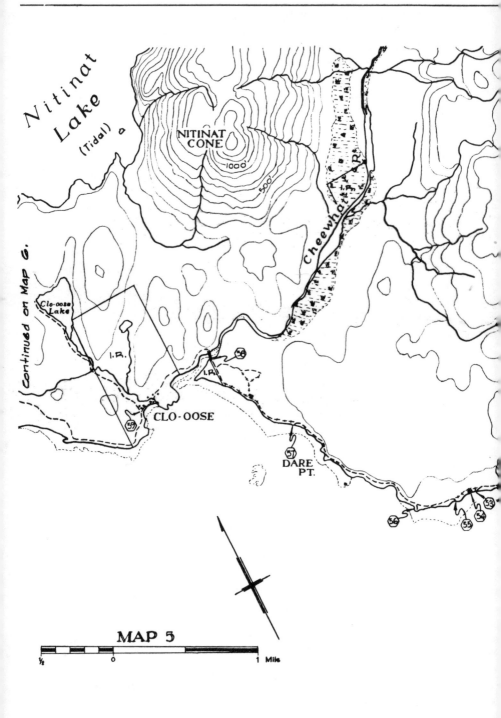

Nitinat Lake *(Tidal)*

NITINAT CONE

—1000'—
500'

Cheewhat R.

I.R.

Continued on Map 6.

Clo-oose Lake

I.R.

56

I.R.

59

CLO-OOSE

57

DARE PT.

58

55

54

53

MAP 5

½   0   1 Mile

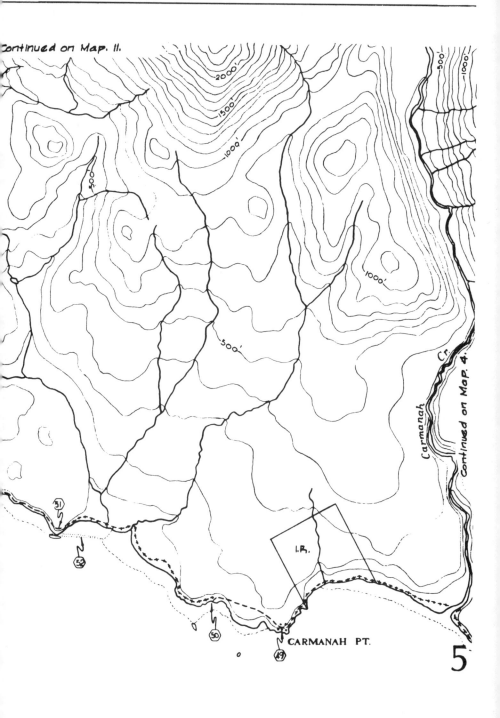

Continued on Map. II.

2000'

1500'

1000'

500'

500'

1000'

1000'

500'

500'

Carmanah Cr.

Continued on Map. 4.

③

②

I.R.

⑤

⑥

CARMANAH PT.

5

(49)   *Carmanah Point Lighthouse. 30 mins. from (43) at low tide, (4) at high trail leaves compound.*

(50)   *Trail from compound joins beach. 20 mins. from (49). 30 mins. to this point from lighthouse by beach (passable at low tide). Continue on beach to (51).*

(51)   *Prominent headland. Trail resumes (preferable to beach). 30 mins. from (45).*

(52)   *"The Cribs", interesting natural breakwater, follow them around headland, if beach route is desired (low tide only).*

(53)   *Trail re-joins beach. 25 mins. from (51).*

(54)   *Department of Transport shack. Good shelter in rain. Water near (50).*

(55)   *Trail resumes. It will branch and re-join, take fork with telephone line. Leave trail at second beach access route (marked by sign).*

(56)   *Sea chasm blocks shelf, rough trail up cliff.*

(57)   *Trail re-joins beach. Follow until a small 2-storey shed is seen in bushes, re-join trail. Follow to (58).*

(58)   *Cheewhat suspension bridge. 50 mins. from (55). Use this crossing.*

(59)   *Intersection with Brown's Bay Trail. Follow telephone line to Whyac.*

It is about one hour from Whyac to the first campsite on the Bamfield side of the Nitinat. You must follow the trail since the shelf is broken by numerous impassable sea chasms. The trail is in good condition and includes most beautiful scenery. Watch especially for the moon rising through the trees and over the cliffs, then reflecting off the ocean waves.

However, you have another option upon reaching Nitinat Narrows, and that is to explore the Nitinat Triangle. To do this, you must arrange to be met by canoes, probably at Brown's Bay. Maps of the Tsusiat and Hobiton drainage systems and Nitinat Lake are included in this guide.

The section of the trail from Nitinat Narrows to the Klanawa River deserves at least one full day because of the many side trips worth making. The hiking is relatively easy, being either along shelf and beach, or along the level cliffs above the beach. The sights to look for are primarily sea formations, such as the Hole-in-the-Wall at (69). Another feature is Tsusiat Falls, which cascades 60 feet over the cliff directly into the ocean. A short way upstream from the falls is the trail bridge across the Tsusiat River. The bridge can be reached by turning towards Port Renfrew at the log ladder from the beach to the cliff at (72). The log ladder must be used because the headland at (73) is impassable. The trail from the Tsusiat to the Klanawa is in good condition, taking only half-an-hour to hike. You will find that your speed improves as you go north because the trail is in better condition than in the southern portions, and you will have become accustomed to hiking after a few days along the trail, and your pack will be lighter than at the beginning, unless you have had the fortune to find a Japanese fishing bulb. Hikers who stagger up the beginning of the trail under a 60-pound albatross and plan to "cut the weight down as I go along" find that the pack weight does not drop considerably unless a great deal of food is brought along and eaten. And of course, thinking hikers pack out all their garbage to help retain the beauty of the trail. Your pack will not lighten quickly, but you will feel better if you pack out your garbage.

The camping facilities at the Klanawa are excellent on both sides of the river. On the Port Renfrew side there is an excellent cabin as well as a beach, and on the Bamfield side there is a large beach. The water in the Klanawa at its mouth is slightly salty. This deep river is best crossed by raft. Sometimes there have been two rafts on the crossing, so hikers could cross the river and still leave a raft on each side.

It is possible to hike all the way from the Klanawa to Bamfield in one day, but it isn't advisable unless you have to meet a deadline. Unless you leave very early in the morning, it is not likely

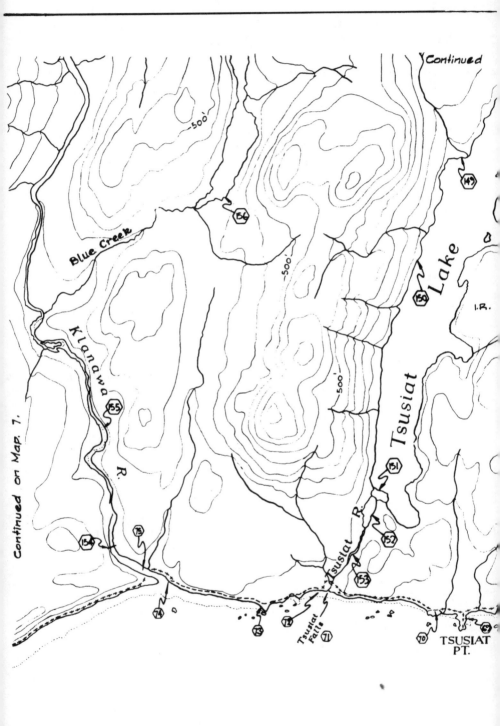

Continued

149

56

Blue Creek

500'

Lake

150

I.R.

Klanawa

Tsusiat

155

151

R.

152

75

Tsusiat R.

153

154

74

72

73

Tsusiat
Falls

71

70

69

TSUSIAT
PT.

Continued on Map. 7.

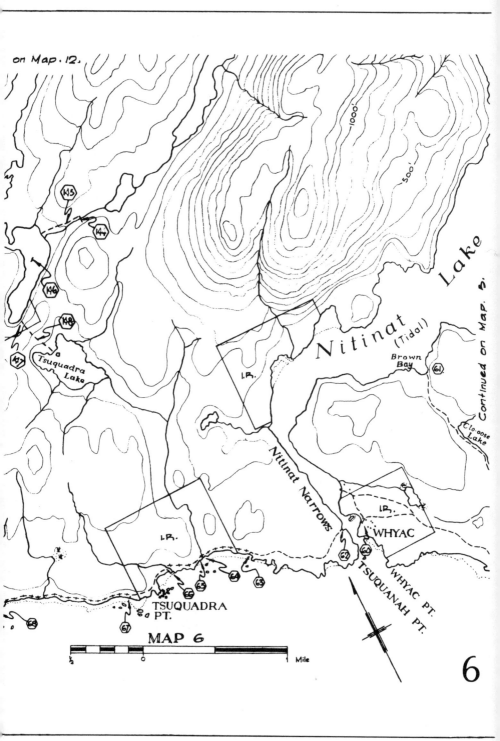

on Map. 12.

1000'

500'

Nitinat Lake

(Tidal)

Brown Bay

61

Continued on Map. 5.

Clooose Lake

145

144

146

148

47

La Tsuquadra Lake

I.R.

Nitinat Narrows

I.R.

WHYAC

WHYAC PT.

TSUQUANAH PT.

62 60

I.R.

65 64 63

TSUQUADRA PT.

66

67

68

MAP 6

½   0   Mile

6

27

(60)   Whyac. Summer residence of some of Nitinat Band. Charge for ferry across Nitinat Narrows usually $2.00 per person. 1½ hours from (58). Often possible to purchase fish and crabs here.

(61)   Brown's Bay, best access to trail from Nitinat Lake.

(62)   Trail resumes on far side of Nitinat Narrows.

(63)   Trail joins beach. 40 mins. from (62).

(64)   Excellent campsite at end of long, fine sand beach.

(65)   Trail resumes by campsite. From here on in, remnants of the old trail can be found. They will be quite overgrown, and should not be depended on to get anywhere. They are good to explore, though.

(66)   Access trail to beach. Tsuquadra Point is to the left as one comes out on the beach. By the point area, fantastic set of wave-worn galleries, well worth exploring. Caves are included in Tsuquadra Reserve, respect them.

(67)   Trail re-joins beach.

(68)   Headland dangerous at high tide, bypass trail available.

(69)   Trail over headland, overgrown side trail leads to Hole-in-the-Wall.

(70)   Trail over headland.

(71)   Tsusiat Falls. 2 hours from (64). Excellent campsite. Some dry caves nearby. Take care at head of falls as rocks very slippery.

(72)   Rejoin trail on steep log ladder. At top, trail to Klanawa begins. In opposite direction, continues short distance to Tsusiat River.

(73)   Impassable headland.

(74)   Trail rejoins beach by Klanawa River. 25 mins. from (71). Excellent cabin just upstream on same side of river.

(144) Waterfall.

(145) Rough trail.

(146) Lagoon, much crabapple around perimeter.

(147) Old trail.

(148) Blowdown area.

(149) (150)   Campsites.

(151) Good campsite, log jam marks creek entrance, carry canoes over log jam.

(152) Little Tsusiat Lake, lots of waterlilies.

(153) River can be waded, very many deadfalls, canoes must be lined down and lifted over some deadfalls. When river is high more lifting required. Allow 1 hour in low water, 2 hours in high water.

(154) About 400 yards upstream there are shallows that can be waded at low tide.

(155) Good canoe water for 2 miles, then rocky and after junction with Blue Creek much logging debris.

(156) Blue Lake, nothing known.

that you would reach Bamfield until late in the evening. For hikers coming from Nitinat, it would be wiser to camp at Darling River or Michigan Creek, both scenes of significant shipwrecks. In fact, the northern part of the trail is where the majority of shipwrecks took place. The remains of many ships will be seen if you explore the beach at low tide. A good book for studying the shipwrecks is Bruce Scott's "Breakers Ahead!" (Review Publishing House, Sidney, B.C.). The book also contains some interesting historical material about the area.

At Michigan Creek you can either follow the trail or follow the beach. The beach access trail just east of Pachena lighthouse is always muddy as well as being steep. The coastline is also difficult, so if in a hurry, you should rejoin the trail at Michigan Creek. The trail from Michigan to the end of Pachena Bay is in excellent condition (better than Stanley park!) but somewhat boring scenically. Remember to sign the register at the lighthouse. Once you reach the lighthouse you will see increasingly such signs of civilization as garbage and people. The gravel road begins at the bible camp at the end of Pachena Bay and leads to Bamfield, where you can reach the main highways by ferry or car.

If stuck in Bamfield waiting for a ferry, you may wish to explore the trails in the vicinity of Cape Beale, but most people have had enough hiking once they reach Bamfield. The nearest suds (soap and beer) are in Port Alberni.

The Cape Beale area has many interesting coves and beaches and spectacular scenery. It is ideal for a weekend visit.

Nitinat Narrows.

Nitinat Lakes

The best approach to the Lakes is from the Knob Point campground on the north side of Nitinat Lake, where there are about 12 prepared campsites. Launch your canoe here and proceed down Nitinat Lake to the mouth of Hobiton Creek. This campsite is not usually crowded, it gives the shortest route to Hobiton Lake, and it avoids the dangerous crossing of Nitinat Lake.

A word of warning is appropriate about Nitinat Lake, firstly it is salt, and secondly, it can be dangerous with high winds. A westerly wind generally sets in about 10:00 a.m. each morning and rapidly builds up a chop. To avoid paddling into this, set off early in the morning. If you time it properly, you will have this wind behind you coming back. The land at the mouth of the Hobiton Creek is an Indian Reserve, please respect it. Although it looks deserted, it is used by the Indians in the fall when the salmon run up Hobiton Creek. The reserve is easily located because it has been logged.

At Hobiton Creek decide whether or not you are to portage the canoe or line it up the creek. Lining up is faster, about 1-1/2 hours, and easier unless the water in the creek is very cold or the flow is very low. Lining up the creek is fairly straight forward, the downstream half has the greater fall and is more rocky. Some of the pools you come to are quite deep and will require paddling across. It is usually better to line down the creek when coming out unless the water is very high.

Hobiton Creek is a gem, the waters are warm in summer and always clear, it is lined by enormous trees and along the banks

31

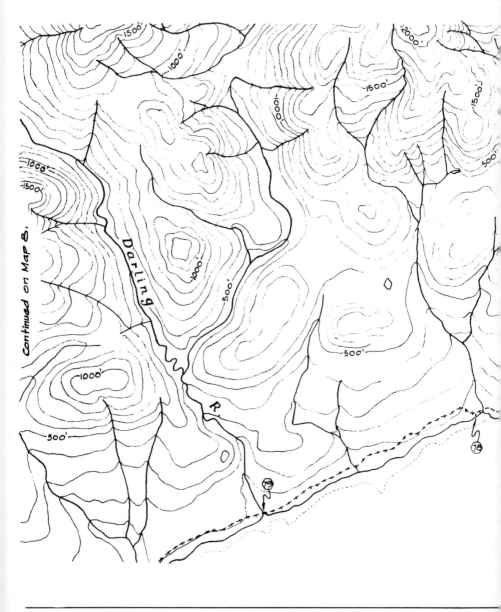

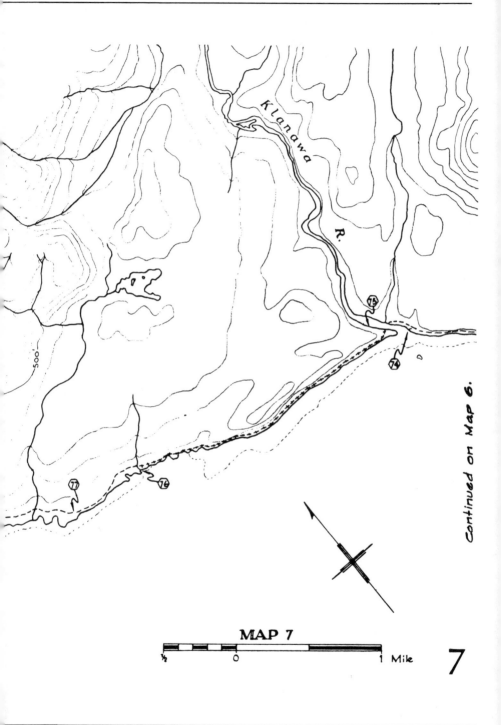

Klanawa R.

75

74

77 76

500'

Continued on Map 6.

MAP 7

½ 0 1 Mile

7

(75)   *Klanawa River. Extremely dangerous, and impassable when high.*

(76)   *Trail resumes by a small waterfall on a prominent fallen tree and is rerouted round a slide.*

(77)   *Small donkey engine.*

(78)   *Trail re-joins beach by stream. 3 hours from (75). Interesting gorge 1/2 mile up creek.*

(79)   *Darling River. Creek impassable when high, except for log some 1/2 mile upstream. Small waterfall upstream. Good campsite.*

there is a wide variety of flowers and shrubs which attracts a rich bird life. Hobiton Creek leaves the lake at a lagoon which is also the end of the portage.

To find the Nitinat Lake end of the portage, paddle to the south end of the Hobiton Reserve, where you will find a rocky point with a large triangular marker used for navigation. The start of the portage is in the little cove beyond the point. You start by walking up a big log.

The portage is rough, as you stumble and sweat along it; don't curse those that cleared it, they were all volunteers, blame governments who will not accept responsibility for recreational development of our land. Allow two hours to complete the portage, which includes one trip with the canoe and one trip with packs.

The portage is characterized by several large deadfalls, mud holes and slippery banks. A two-man carry is advised but a single man can carry a canoe across.

From the end of the portage at the lagoon, there is a very attractive view of the north shore of Hobiton Lake. Most of the campsites on the lake are scattered along the north side and three that are popular are shown on the map. The Dead Alder site has room for 5 tents or so, and has some enormous cedar trees; Hitchie Creek site can take 8 tents; Cedar Log site can take 8 tents.

The flat at the mouth of Hitchie Creek provides a very open site which is a godsend when there are mosquitoes as the wind blows them away. Hitchie Creek has a very attractive canyon, and the few visitors to Hitchie Lake report that it also is attractive, however, do not try to reach it by going through the woods, walk up the stream bed to the falls then cut around through the woods to the top.

The Cedar Log site is at the mouth of a little creek and is marked by a large log projecting horizontally over the water. From this campsite it takes about 1 hour to climb up Hobiton Ridge through the old trees. There are no trails up the ridge as yet, but passage is easy if you keep out of the gullies. The forest is very open and largely carpeted with fern. Both Hitchie Creek and Cedar Log campsites offer excellent swimming as there is a steep drop-off at each one.

The Cedar Log camp makes a good jumping off point for Squalicum Lake. The Squalicum trail starts at a small gravel beach on the south shore of Hobiton about half a mile to the east of the camp. The entrance to the trail is marked by red ribbon and lies below a saddle in the ridge.

The trail between Squalicum and Hobiton rises 400 feet and is very steep. Canoes have been taken over it, but it is not recommended unless you feel you really must, and then have at least 3

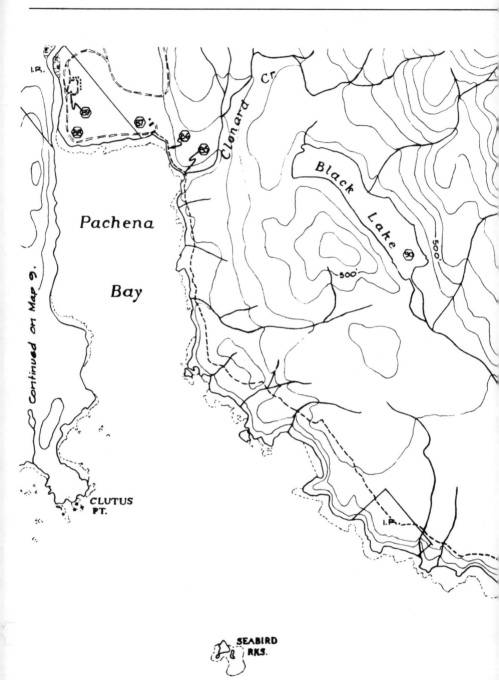

Pachena

Bay

Clonard Cr.

Black Lake

500'

500'

I.R.

Continued on Map 9.

CLUTUS
PT.

I.R.

SEABIRD
RKS.

Continued on Map. 7.

MAP

PACHENA PT.

½   0   1 Mile

8

(80)   Michigan Creek. Good campsite. 20 mins. from (79). Trail begins on bridge over creek and is good but a bit overgrown.

(81)   Beach access trail. At best, a quagmire.

(82)   Pachena Point Lighthouse, sign in to establish usage of trail.

(83)   Sea lion colony, March-May.

(84)   Beach access trail.

(85)   Old cabin, leaks in rain.

(86)   End of West Coast Trail.

(87)   Camp Ross, a bible camp.

(88)   Anacla Park commercial camp ground.

(89)   Grocery store and service station.

people to help. A feature of the trail is the number of enormous mossy trees along it.

Squalicum Lake is very scenic, from its western end Squalicum Creek runs westward through two small lakes to discharge into Tsusiat Lake. At present this creek is not well known, but a few people have travelled down it by rubber raft. There is a 30-foot high waterfall about 1-1/2 miles up from Tsusiat Lake.

The entrance to the portage between Hobiton and Tsusiat is on the south shore a little to the east of the end of Hobiton Lake and is marked by a large log sloping into the Lake, and tape. The portage is rough, with large deadfalls, mudholes and slippery banks. It is much easier with a two-man carry, and even then it will take about 1-1/2 hours to carry a canoe over it. With a pack the portage takes about 45 minutes. Again, this portage was scouted and cleared and is steadily being improved by volunteers from Vancouver Island.

The portage passes beside a very pretty bog lying on the crest of the ridge. As well as the usual flowers, sundews, the insectivorous plants, are quite readily found in the mossy sections of the bog. Watch for them after rain when the light glitters on the rain drops held on their petals and you will see how they earned their name.

As you approach Tsusiat, note how the trees become smaller, but the forest still remains open and easy to traverse except in the gullies and along the lake shores which have a growth of crabapple and salal which is very difficult to penetrate.

The portage comes to the east end of Tsusiat Lake where there is a poor campsite which is very boggy and where movement is hindered by extensive groves of crabapple, however, enough space has been cleared to provide camping space for a small group.

Tsusiat Lake has a very different character to Hobiton Lake. Hobiton Ridge still dominates the view but it is now much farther away. The timber along the shores is smaller, and there are some interesting islands with examples of stunted growth.

If there is no wind, it will take one to one and a half hours to paddle to the western end. About halfway along the south shore, near the little island, you will see the narrow entrance to the lagoon. This sheltered spot was used by the Nitinat Band in former times as a place of refuge when they were being harried by enemies. The lagoon is shallow and usually warm, a good place for a dip.

The large grove of Cedar trees on the point between the lagoon and the lake is on Reserve land. It is said that it was from these trees that the Nitinat Band used to select their canoe logs, from here they would float them down Tsusiat Lake to the coast.

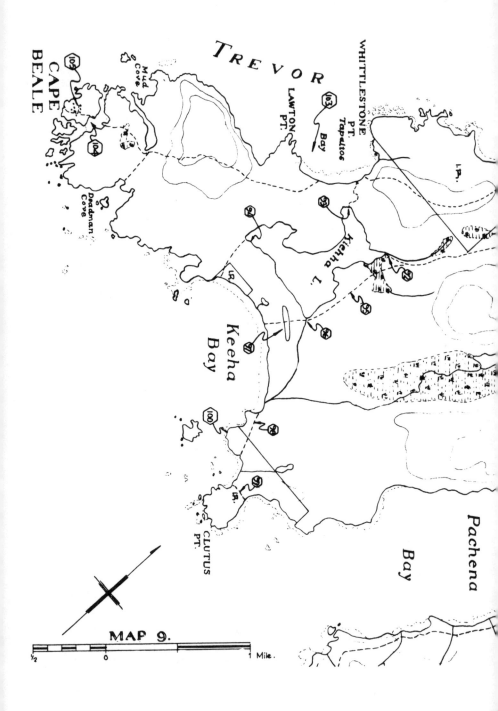

MAP 9.

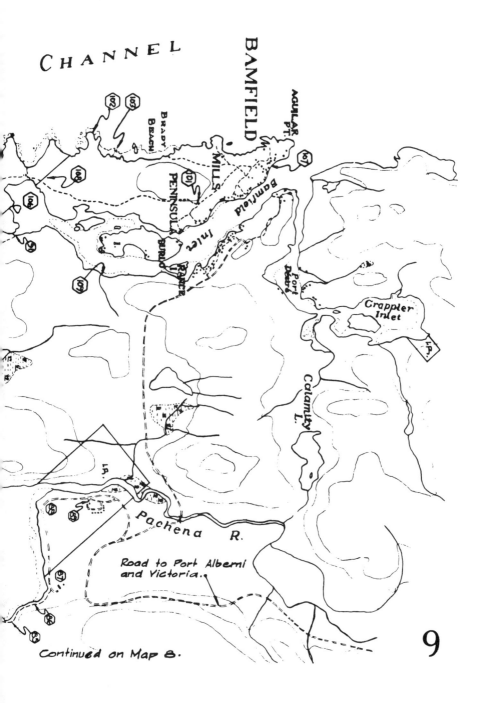

CHANNEL

BAMFIELD

AGUILAR PT.

BRADY BEACH

MILLS

PENINSULA

Bamfield Inlet

BURLO PLACE

Port Distr.

Crappler Inlet

Calamity L.

Pachena R.

Road to Port Alberni
and Victoria.

Continued on Map 8.

9

(90)	Black Lake is scenic, has good fishing, status of trail access uncertain. Elk are now established around lake.
(91)	Start of trail.
(92)	(93) (94) Boats usually at these points, but not guaranteed, return when possible and treat gently.
(95)	Very rough trail to use when boats unavailable.
(96)	Beaver dam.
(97)	Cabins here are disguised but in good condition.
(98)	(99) Trails across headlands, respect Indian Reservation lands.
(100)	If shore route is chosen, it leads through arch with deep pool under.
(101)	Start of main Cape Beale Trail.
(102)	Execution Rock, scene of slaughter of captives in past.
(103)	Attractive bay.
(104)	This channel dries at low tide.
(105)	Cape Beale Lighthouse.
(106)	Extensive mud flats at low tide.
(107)	Lady Rose berths on west side of inlet. Hitch a lift across on a boat.
(108)	Trail becomes overgrown.
(109)	Beach walkable at low tide.

A trail to Tsuquadra Lake leaves from the south-west tip of the lagoon but it is very overgrown, the passage to Tsuquadra taking about 40 minutes. Tsuquadra has not been explored to any extent as yet, the possibility exists that the creek draining it may give an easy lining channel which would take you quite close to Nitinat Narrows thus making a circuitous trip easier. Almost certainly the creek will have much deadfall across it as no clearing has been done. A trail leads from the lagoon up Squalicum Creek to the Falls, but is very rough. Allow 1½ hours. The best campsite on Tsusiat is at the west end near the log jam marking the outflow from the lake.

To continue to the sea, pull the canoe over the log jam and move into Little Tsusiat Lake and enter the Tsusiat River, which is quite shallow. Passage on the river is slow because of the large numbers of fallen trees across it. If you are determined and the river is not too high, it is possible to take canoes down to the top of the Tsusiat Falls. If you are easily frustrated, leave your canoe, and walk down the creek bed as the bush on either side is exceptionally dense. A word of warning, the rocks at the lip of the Falls are very slick.

A trail may have been cut along the north bank of Tsusiat Creek but its status is unknown.

The Life Saving, or West Coast Trail crosses the Tsusiat just before the Falls, and one hundred yards north of the bridge there is a good beach access trail. Some have taken their canoes down here and travelled by the sea to Nitinat Narrows, however, do not depend on being able to do this as it is safe only on an exceptionally calm sea. It is also unsafe to attempt to pass Nitinat Narrows except in the very short period of slack at the turn of the tide. If you try the sea passage take care to avoid the currents and waves over Nitinat Bar.

When travelling on these lakes, always remember, and allow for, the effects of contrary winds. In general, Hobiton Lake can be enjoyed in a two-day week end, while to reach and explore Tsusiat takes three days; if you are determined to reach the sea from Tsusiat, allow four days until such time as portages and trails are improved.

This account of the Nitinat Lake Chain is sketchy because much exploration has still to be done. If you travel off the main lakes, and find places of interest, please inform the Sierra Club of British Columbia at 1572 Monterey Avenue, Victoria, because such information is needed to build up a strong case for preservation of the Nitinat Lakes.

Trail bridge over Tsusiat River.

Access to the Trail and Nitinat Lakes

There is no public transport to take you to or from the West Coast Trail and Nitinat except the 'Lady Rose' which operates as a ferry between Bamfield and Port Alberni. All other routes require the use of logging roads established by the forest companies and are subject to various restrictions. In essence, passage over the roads must be confined to outside working hours, that is from 6:00 p.m. to 6:00 a.m. and all day during the weekends. There must be no overnight camping except at designated camping sites while on company administered forest land. Each forest company will provide maps of the logging roads it maintains and travellers are advised to obtain these as some of the interlinks are quite complex. The companies involved are MacMillan Bloedel, B.C. Forest Products and Crown Zellerbach. While the companies claim that these are private roads, this is only where they cross private land. The logging roads were built by the companies, but, in general, on the Tree Farm Licences the cost was allowed to be deducted from revenue paid to the Government for use of the timber. So for the safety of all concerned, co-operation on travel restrictions is essential, but do not let yourself be harrassed into believing that you have no right to be on the roads.

Access to Port Renfrew can be made from Victoria by way of Sooke and Jordan River, and from Duncan by way of Shawnigan Lake and the San Juan valley road.

To reach the start of the trail from Port Renfrew it is necessary to cross the Gordon River. At present this can be done only by boat as described earlier, but a bridge is to be built by B.C. Forest Products (BCFP) which will ease access.

To use the Nitinat Lakes or to reach the trail at its mid point, access must be by way of the head of Nitinat Lake. From Victoria drive through Duncan and Lake Cowichan to Youbou, where you leave the blacktop. Take the North Shore road from there to the head of Lake Cowichan. At the head, turn left and follow the sign for Caycuse; do not go to the Crown Zellerbach (CZ) Nitinat Camp. After rising over the divide you will drop into the Nitinat Valley, and eventually come to a major T junction. If you look right at this junction you will see an old wooden truss bridge which carries the Port Alberni road to the Nitinat. At this junction a sign post indicates that the Nitinat Campsite created by MacMillan Bloedel (MB) and BCFP is to the left.

If you require boat transport to the mouth of Nitinat Lake turn left and travel down the south side of the valley. This will take you to the Reserve of the Nitinat Band who will usually ferry you down the lake for a fee of about $20.00 per boatload, and a little farther on to the very pleasant Nitinat campsite where you may leave your car and launch your boat if you intend to go straight down Nitinat Lake.

If you wish to go to Hobiton and Tsusiat Lakes, it is better to turn right at the T junction, cross the bridge and make a big loop around to the north side of the Nitinat Valley, after one mile a sign post indicates the road to the Knob Point campsite which lies seven miles down the road. This campsite is a better start for Hobiton because it minimizes the time required on Nitinat Lake and avoids having to paddle across the Lake. The campsite is pleasant, and has a resident pine marten, so ensure you hang up your food. The logging road at Knob Point continues almost to Hobiton Creek but is badly washed out and in 1972 was impassable.

The head of Nitinat Lake may be reached directly from Nanaimo, Port Alberni and Bamfield by logging roads. From Nanaimo drive south on the Island Highway until you see the sign for Nanaimo Lakes and Green Mountain, turn west and follow this to the start of CZ's Nanaimo Lakes operation at First Lake. As this road is gated at the summit you must stop here and pick up a key from the watchman. Continue towards Fourth Lake, take the right hand fork half a mile before Fourth Lake and continue to a point where four roads meet, take the left hand road until it forks, take the right hand fork, not road M29, cross the summit, locking the gate behind you, and follow the road down to CZ's Nitinat Camp. From here cut back to the junction of the Caycuse and Cowichan North Shore roads and continue as previously described. The key may be handed in at CZ's Nitinat Camp or retained for the return journey when it can be given to the watchman at First Lake.

This road is a very short route but crosses the Island Range at a high elevation and is often not free of snow at the summit until June. It is not usable early in the year. It is also a very rough stretch from Fourth Lake to the summit, so use your judgement regarding its use.

From Port Alberni take the MB roads posted for Bamfield, keep going through Franklin River until you see the sign posts for Nitinat, follow these past the Flora Lake Main Line Road to the Knob Point turnoff and the Nitinat Bridge.

To reach Bamfield from Victoria, go first to the T junction near the Nitinat Bridge, turn right and follow the road to the point where the Flora Lake Main Line takes off westward, follow this to Bamfield. From Port Alberni go through Franklin River and follow the sign posts for Sarita Lake and Bamfield.

From Bamfield it is possible to drive to Pachena Bay and from there to explore Cape Beale or move down the trail.

A southerly side road off the Flora Lake Main will take you into the Klanawa Valley giving access to the wild country at the mouth of Klanawa River.

Another way to reach Bamfield from Port Alberni is on the ferry 'Lady Rose' which leaves Port Alberni at 8:00 a.m. on Tuesdays and Thursdays arriving at Bamfield at 12:00 noon and leaves Bamfield at 1:00 p.m. on Tuesdays and Thursdays arriving at Port Alberni at 4:00 p.m.

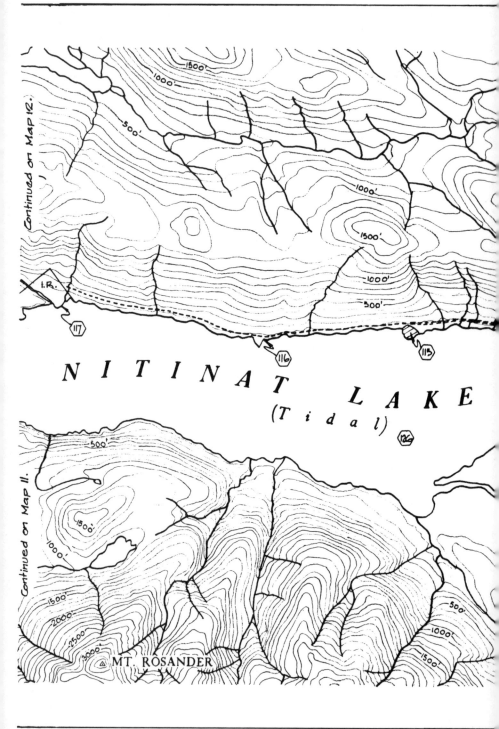

Continued on Map 12.

I.R.

117

116

113

126

N I T I N A T   L A K E
(T i d a l)

Continued on Map 11.

MT. ROSANDER

MAP 10

½   0   1 Mile

10

(110)   Good canoe water up to Nitinat Falls.

(111)   Standing waves at mouth.

(112)   Sandy beach and driftwood.

(113)   M.B. and B.C.F.P. Nitinat campsite.

(114)   Road to Knob Point.

(115)   B.C.F.P. Knob Point campsite.

(116)   B.C.F.P. logging road to Hobiton, presently impassable beyond Knob Point.

(117)   Hobiton Indian Reserve, good beach, respect privacy and property. Reserve identified by being clear-cut.

Pointers

Even under the most adverse conditions imaginable, hiking the West Coast Trail can be an enjoyable experience if you are properly prepared. On the other hand, improper equipment can turn an otherwise perfect hike into a nightmare. You should prepare for the worst, and the worst on the west coast of Vancouver Island is beyond what most people have experienced. Cold winds and torrential rains are hard enough to bear by themselves but they are usually combined with slippery logs, muddy paths and high rivers. Add blisters, fogged glasses and wet clothes and you have a good recipe for misery. Fortunately, most of the bad weather occurs in winter but summer hikers should plan on rain at least every second day. If it is warm and wet you will also encounter mosquitoes. And then there are wet sleeping bags. And broken packs. And a thousand other things waiting to ruin a hike.

The following list of things to take is intended only as a guide. You should look for principles instead of items. The lists are the same for men and women.

Most packs taken on the West Coast Trail weigh between 35 and 55 pounds. A pack with 40 pounds of equipment and food, if wisely chosen, can be sufficient to last up to 10 days.

There are four types of equipment needed on a normal hike. General equipment includes such things as tent and packs, clothing includes such things as boots and rain gear, cooking/eating includes such things as frying pans and cups. Miscellaneous includes such items as pencil and paper, cameras and cards.

General equipment consists of all the hardware necessary to

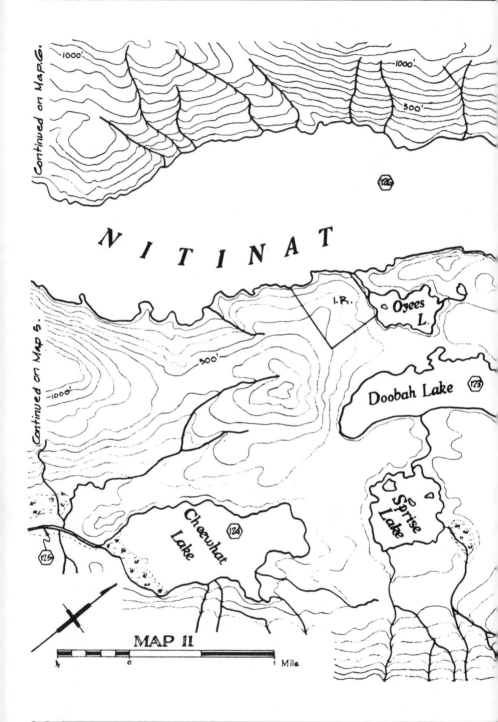

Continued on Map G.

1000'
1000'
500'
126

N I T I N A T

I.R.
Oyees L.
500'
-1000'
Continued on Map 5.
Doobah Lake
173

Cheewhat Lake
124
Sprise Lake
125

MAP II

½   0   1 Mile

L A K E

I.R.

1000'
500'
1000'

I.R.

Marchand Cr.

Doobah

1000'
1500'
2000'
2500'
3000'

1500'
2000'
1500'

11

(118)   *Start of portage in cove to west of point with triangular marker on it.*

(119)   *Mouth of Hobiton Creek, if Indians fishing salmon in fall, use portage.*

(120)   *Portage trail rough, allow 1 hour for carrying canoe.*

(121)   *Waterfall.*

(122)   *Good camping beaches.*

(123)   *Much logging around these lakes, not much visited.*

(124)   *Cheewhat Lake is wintering area for trumpeter swans.*

(125)   *Salmon run in Cheewhat all year round.*

(126)   *Caution! Keep close to shore on Nitinat, winds get up suddenly and are predominantly westerly after 10 a.m. Nitinat Lake is cold if your canoe tips, you will suffer from exposure. Nitinat Lake also full of jelly fish in some seasons. Watch for seals and otters.*

maintain you. The following list gives a good guide for initial planning:

pack
tent
sleeping bag
groundsheet
matches
fire starter
axe
knife
file or stone
spare parts and tools for repairs
50 feet of rope
tide tables
flashlight and spare batteries
candles
compass
watch
maps
toiletries
first aid kit
mosquito repellent

Most of the above equipment is essential but some economizing can be made by sharing certain pieces of equipment within a group. For example, it is silly for a group of eight people to take along eight double tents and eight axes and eight sets of tide tables. At the same time, eight people would be foolish to depend on only 50 feet of rope. The principle then is to make sure that the group has enough equipment for all. If the group plans to split up into smaller groups, as many do at Clo—oose, then both groups should have a full set of equipment.

Regarding packs, a moderately-priced aluminum frame pack is both strong and light, while wooden packs are heavier but easier to repair. The pack covering should be waterproof and the pack should ride high on the back.

The best tents are the lightweight waterproof ones. Because of the heavy rains on the trail, it is wise to take along plastic sheets for both the top and bottom of the tent.

Sleeping bags are usually worth what you pay for them. If you can afford a good one you will have a more comfortable sleep than if you take a cheap one. The minimum specifications for a bag should be quick-drying, light and effective to about freezing temperature.

Matches should be waterproofed with wax and stored in a dry place in the pack. Safety matches are useless. Firestarter (either liquid or the solid white product similar to napalm) is essential since almost all the wood along the trail is wet or green. Newsprint tends to absorb moisture as well as being unneccessary weight.

The axe should be long-handled for chopping logs (hatchets are useless for heavy chopping) but only one is needed per group. A hatchet is useful for kindling and banging nails into rafts. Nails can either be carried along or pulled from driftwood.

Spare parts should depend upon what kind of pack is taken along, but thick string has a variety of uses, including spare boot laces. If a metal pack is taken, wire and pliers are a good safety precaution.

The length of rope required is determined by the width of the rivers that must be rafted. A working return system can be set up with about 200 feet of 1/4-inch rope, and another 100 feet is useful for securing logs on the raft or if a stream is high and requires more than 200 feet of rope to cross. A total of 300 feet per group is usually sufficient for rafting the Walbran and Klanawa rivers, the two that are best crossed on rafts.

Maps, compass, tide tables and a watch are all necessary. The trail is usually marked by the old telephone wire or plastic, but if you lose the trail it is often difficult to regain. Candles are useful in the cabins and flashlights are essential on windy nights.

Toiletries are considered a luxury by some hikers and a necessity by others. Eye makeup is a silly luxury but other items such as toothpaste are a matter of preference. Toilet paper has a variety of uses and a full roll will last about seven days.

Mosquito repellent is needed only in warm, wet weather. The liquid drop variety is light. Garlic is rumoured to be a repellent. Another solution is to camp in open areas where the wind blows mosquitoes away. Tents with netting are essential in certain areas.

Clothing should be chosen for warmth, weight and usefulness. It is also a matter of personal preference. Some people need a set of clean clothes every morning, while others prefer to wear the same clothes every day and leave room in the pack for items such as cameras or canned bacon. Again, the following list is a guide:

boots with Vibram soles
socks
jeans
waterproof overalls
shorts
underwear
undershirts

warm shirt or sweater
warm jacket
waterproof overcoat
rain hat (especially if you wear glasses)
gloves

Many of the older guides to the trail suggested hikers use cleated boots. However, most of the slippery logs have balance wires now and can be crossed as safely with Vibram soles. Vibram soled boots are also good for hiking on rocks and are more adaptable than cleated boots. The boots should be of waterproof leather and have cushioned insoles. Like sleeping bags, boots are usually worth what you pay for them. A few dollars more can be the difference between pleasant hiking and blistered misery.

Good socks also can help prevent blisters. Wearing a thin pair of nylon socks inside a pair of thick wool socks cuts down on chafing. Clean dry socks are preferable to wet socks so hikers usually take two or three spare pairs. However, if the inside of the boot gets wet, dry socks will soon get wet from seepage.

Coveralls or some form of rain gear are essential to a pleasant hike. The nylon varieties are excellent at shedding water but tend to rip at the seams. The plastic coveralls also increase body heat by collecting sweat on the inside of the garment. This can cause a chill when you suddenly stop hiking.

A hat is useful for keeping hair dry, but not a necessity if a towel is brought along. However, a peaked hat such as a baseball cap is useful in rain if you wear glasses. Hiking with fogged glasses is difficult and often results in falls. A spare set of glasses is a good precaution.

Cooking/Eating. No matter what kind of diet you plan for the hike, you will need some equipment with which to cook and eat. The equipment you take is best chosen in relation to your diet but a large pot for boiling water seems to be a necessity. Likewise, frying is a good way of cooking rough meals, so a frying pan should be taken along. After that, items such as cups, plates and spoons are also worth packing.

frying pan
pot lifter
large pot with lid
small pot with lid, or small kettle
cup
plate
bowl
fork and spoon

can opener (if canned goods taken)
butane burner
plastic garbage bags
foil
scrubber
water bottle

The frying pan should be large and capable of withstanding high temperatures. The ones that come with several other pieces of camping equipment (all for a low, low price) soon demonstrate why they sell for a low, low price. Highly recommended are the teflon-coated frying pans with collapsible handles and a lid. The lid keeps ashes out of the ham and the teflon makes the pan easy to clean in cold water with no soap. A good frying pan is worth its space in the pack as it will produce better meals than a cheap pan. The lifter for the frying pan is an unnecessary item, a fork or a spoon can be used instead for everything except fresh eggs.

The large pot is useful for big groups since it cooks such things as porridge, rice, noodles and mussels (more about these later). The small pot is good for quick boiling and supplementary dishes such as soup.

A cup is needed and so is a plate, but the lid of a pot can often double as a dish and bowl. A spoon is a necessity but the fork can be replaced by a pair of hand-carved chop sticks.

A butane burner is a good idea for small groups but it is heavy and bulky. A burner does not give off enough heat to dry clothes and should be used to cook on only when a fire is unsuitable, or as is more likely, impossible.

Miscellaneous equipment is the stuff you'd like to take but really shouldn't because it is too heavy and you don't really need it. But almost everyone takes at least one such item. A lot depends on your experience, strength and pack size. What you take also depends on your interests. If you have a camera fetish and leave your camera at home, you could spend seven days kicking yourself over all the once-in-a-lifetime shots you are missing. If you plan to take things easy, a deck of cards can be a good pastime as well as a device for keeping groups together. If you are a philosopher or poet, take along pencil and paper. (Pens tend to malfunction.) If you like reading, take along a book, especially one on hiking or wilderness foods. Another "extra" is a fishing rod but very few people catch anything other than sniffles along the trail. The best possibilities are probably in the ocean or at the mouth of the Gordon and in Nitinat Narrows. A compact spin-casting rig would be most suitable. (If you fish, don't forget that the southern banks of the Gordon and Nitinat are Indian Reserves.)

Looking east from log jam at west end of Tsusiat Lake, Hobiton Ridge in rear.

Cedar Log camp, Hobiton Lake.

To conclude the section on equipment, you should realize that most of your pack's weight and bulk will be taken up by equipment. Most of the equipment listed here is essential, but pack weight can be cut down drastically if, before leaving, groups work out arrangements for sharing equipment.

Food is another item that should be taken on a group basis. If it is not at least partially shared it raises the possibility of everyone bringing along a salt shaker, sugar, rice and many other items that can take up valuable space just by their packaging in small quantities. Sharing goods has the added advantage of increasing group identity, something that is often taxed by seven days of close living.

The principle in selecting food to take is to choose foods with high energy but low weight. Thus dried foods are ideal and starches are a necessity. Meat is a difficult item to take and should be stored properly.

The following list is a guide. The ham, for example, can be changed to beef, and the starches are a matter of personal preference, though rice and noodles are easy to cook.

        roast, especially boneless ham
        salami
        dried meat, such as shrimp
        mussels (from the beach)
        dried peas
        dried soups
        wild plants (if you know which ones to choose)
        rice
        noodles
        instant potatoes
        heavy bread, rye or pumpernickel
        porridge
        margarine (will not go off like butter)
        sugar
        orange crystals
        coffee/tea
        eggs (fresh or powdered)
        canned bacon (if ham not taken)
        cheese
        scrogin (described later)
        fruit (fresh and dried)
        sauces and seasonings
        pancake mix (or similar)

A ham roast is useful because it can be used in all three meals, but it should not be stored in plastic, wrap it in waxed paper and several layers of thick brown paper. A smoked ham will keep at least seven days and is thus highly recommended. Salamis (whole) keep well and are good with cheese for a quick lunch. They can be used as a bacon substitute or chopped up into a spaghetti. The garlic in certain salamis has limited success at repelling mosquitoes.

Dried meats such as shrimp are lightweight and easy to prepare. A good place to buy dried foods is a Chinese grocery store. Dried mushrooms can make a dull meal into an interesting one. The following recipe for West Coast Trail Fried Rice is nutritious, easy to prepare and tasty.

"Boil dried mushrooms and dried shrimps until texture is soft (about 25 minutes). Boil some rice slowly with lid on for about 25 minutes (Chinese style, no peeking). Boil dried peas until ready to eat. Drain and dry shrimps and mushrooms; allow rice to cool. Take frying pan, melt margarine and begin frying sliced mushrooms (make sure stems are off) and shrimps. Other meat ingredients such as ham or mussels can also be added here. Add rice and stir thoroughly. Add peas and any other vegetables and keep stirring. Add soy sauce (if any) and serve."

Dried soups are good because they are easy to prepare and amenable to added ingredients such as ham bits or wild plants. Rice, especially brown rice, is filling and adaptable to several recipes. Noodles are tasty in combination with ready-made sauces and cheese.

Bread should be heavy so it won't break up in the pack and does not waste valuable space. Porridge gives a warm, solid start to a day's hiking, and is simple to prepare (add water and boil). Orange juice that comes in the form of crystals gives a psychological lift in the morning. Fresh eggs are difficult to pack without breaking but sometimes worth the effort. Canned bacon is a luxury the whole group could indulge in one morning.

Coffee and/or tea are valuable sources of warmth and energy on cold days and are particularly good with lots of sugar. You might try premixing coffee with powdered chocolate, powdered milk and brown sugar to save mixing it on the trail. It works. Powdered milk is also good sprinkled directly on porridge. If you don't like powdered milk in tea learn to like it the Russian way with a few drops of lemon juice.

Scrogin is a mixture of chocolate chips, raisins and salted peanuts. The name, according to a New Zealander, originated in New Zealand. The mixture is an excellent source of energy while hiking. The sugar in the chocolate gives energy, the salt cuts down

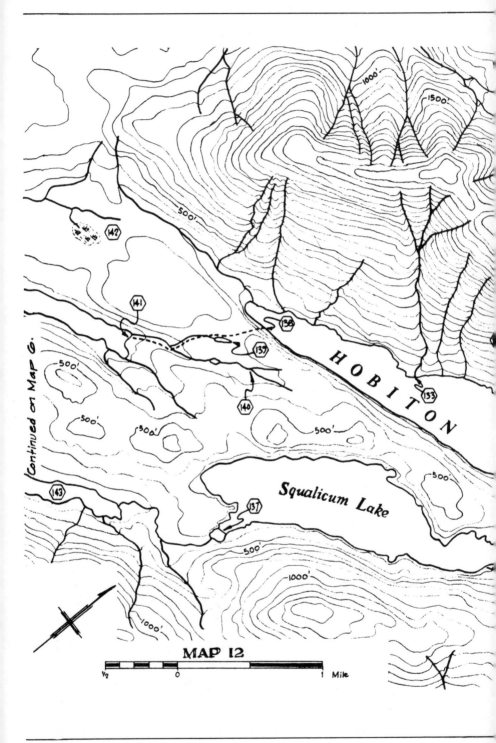

Continued on Map G.

142

141

136

139

140

133

H O B I T O N

143

137

Squalicum Lake

500'
500'
500'
500'
500'
500'
500'
500'
500'
1000'
1000'
1000'
1000'
1500'

MAP 12

½   0   1 Mile

LAKE

Hitchie Lake

2000'
500'
1500'
1000'
500'
1000'
1500'
2000'
2500'
2500'
500'
500'
1000'
1500'
500'
1000'

134
134
131
132
130
129
128
127

Continued on Map 10

12

(127)	Pools in upper reaches of creek.
(128)	Dead Alder Campsite.
(129)	Hitchie Creek campsite.
(130)	Canyon.
(131)	Waterfall.
(132)	Boundary of initial logging planned by B.C.F.P.
(133)	Cedar Log campsite.
(134)	Trail to Squalicum Lake, steep and rough, start marked by tape.
(135)	Forest open and easy going on ridges, magnificent trees.
(136)	Hobiton Ridge.
(137)	Log jam.
(138)	Portage entrance on sloping log, marked by tape. Portage rough with mudholes and much deadfall.
(139)	Sphagnum bog, good flower spot.
(140)	Gorge.
(141)	Limited campsite, poor and boggy.
(142)	Swamps.
(143)	Little Squalicum Lake.

on sweating and the raisins probably have all sorts of vitamins your mother told you about.

Sauces and seasonings are an important part of the food list since they can make bland food into something worth eating. And the nature of the hike means taking along bland food. This heading includes such things as salt, pepper, garlic, soy sauce, tomato sauce and gravy.

And finally, the mussels. These are the blue-shelled bivalves that grow in great numbers on rocks near the low tide level. They are edible at all times except when there is a red tide in the area. (If you don't know what red tide is, you'd be wise to leave the mussels alone.) They can be eaten several ways, including boiling them in the shell until the shells open and then taking the meat out and eating it with margarine and salt. An alternative is to chop them up and fry them. People eating mussels should be careful to avoid pearls. As yet the mussel beds show no sign of being depleted by hikers.

To conclude the section on food, a note on the water is appropriate since almost all of the above items depend on water. All the water along the trail is safe to drink but some streams are safer to drink from than others. The slow-moving trickles in the bogs probably have high bacteria counts and if used could result in diarrhea a few days later. Some of the water bodies such as Nitinat, Cheewhat, Klanawa and Walbran are partially salt water and thus unsuitable for drinking. But apart from these the water along the West Coast Trail is generally delicious.

Ferns carpet the forest floor on Hobiton Ridge.

Wildlife

It is unusual to see many large animals along the trail or in the Nitinat Lakes. The forest and bush make it very easy for them to hide. However, deer, bear, cougar and the very rare Vancouver Island wolf, have all been seen in the area. Sea lions are often seen at their rocks near Pachena. Seals and otters are common in Nitinat Lake.

Ironically it is the small animals that can cause you anguish; mice, ground squirrels and pine martens are inveterate robbers of packs if left on the ground overnight. To avoid loss and spoilage of food, hang food packs every night. Many campsites have a resident marten. These small animals are quite tame, having had little contact with man. Try to keep them that way.

Bird life is rich, eagles abound, loons, mergansers, ducks and other acquatic birds are common. The rare Trumpeter Swan winters on the marshes of the Cheewhat, and can be seen from late fall to early spring.

Fishing is usually more rewarding in the sea but the lakes and streams have trout. Sockeye, chum, and spring salmon run into Hobiton Lake. The fish in this system are interesting in that they spawn in gravel along the lake perimeter particularly at the mouths of creeks, rather than in stream beds. If you are in the area in the fall, allow for this when choosing your campsite.

Sockeye run into the Cheewhat system, this race is unusual because the spawners return throughout the year rather than in a concerted rush. This was obviously of great importance to the early Indian settlements.

The chum fishery of the Doobah was the richest on the coast until eliminated by early overfishing and by some very crude logging done by subcontractors to B.C. Forest Products which filled the stream bed with debris and scoured out the gravel. The Doobah used to be as pretty as the Hobiton. There is no beauty left there now.

If you fish, the creek mouths are reported to be the best locations either along the coast or in the lakes, and also Nitinat Narrows.

Shell fish are available along the seashore, just now there are many mussels and clams, but remember how the Long Beach clams were depleted, and only take enough to satisfy you. Conservation extends to more than trees.

Linesman's cabin at the Klanawa.

Indian Lands

Three separate groups of Indians live along the West Coast Trail, the most southerly is at Port Renfrew, the Nitinat Band has its lands in the Nitinat Basin, and the Ohiat Band has its lands at Pachena Bay and around Cape Beale.

These Bands have several reserves along the trail and near the lakes, some are inhabited and some not. Those that are inhabited are at Port Renfrew, Clo—oose, Whyac, Hobiton River, Pachena Bay, and around Nitinat Lake. All the reserve lands are clearly marked on the maps. Some reserves are only inhabited seasonally so do not assume that if no one is there that the buildings are abandoned and that you have licence to enter them, or use their utensils. Remember that the reserves are private land. Even though the trail may cross the reserves your use of it is only through the courtesy of the Indians. Your rights do not include camping on the reserve lands, or use of their wood unless you have obtained consent from Band members.

Some of the reserves carry traces of very early settlement, these must be treated with respect and not interfered with for they are of particular importance to the Bands.

Remember that all hikers along the trail are dependent on the Indians at Port Renfrew and Whyac for ferry services, and that in the future the success of park status for the trail will depend on the willing co-operation of the Bands. Therefore, please ensure that you respect their lands and property, and advise other hikers, who may be unaware of the status of reserve lands, to do the same.

Tsusiat Falls.

Hot Tips

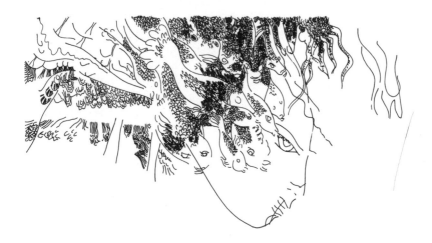

Now that your pack is full of good things to take and good things to eat, you're almost ready to leave for the hike. But there's a lot more to the hike than maps and boots. Seven days, the average time needed to hike the West Coast Trail, may sound like a short period in the city but out on the trail, where you may not see anyone for a day or two, the seven days become a long time. And generally the near-wilderness situation requires learning a whole new set of attitudes. People will find the smallest things annoying, such as your best friend's habit of whistling off key. Normally, you don't notice the habit but after seven days of continual contact you begin to think maybe your friend is doing it on purpose just to bother you.

Which raises the question of group sizes. The minimum is three since if one hiker is injured the other two can look after him and go for help. But a group of three is difficult to keep on friendly terms. Groups of three tend to fracture into two good friends and a third person. Naturally the third person begins to feel left out, and a lonely feeling in the wilderness is like no other lonely feeling. It often leads to irrational actions.

Four is a good group size because it is small but still balanced. Groups of five or six are also good if they stay together but with so many people they often break into smaller groups simply because of different hiking rates or different due dates. And then trouble can occur.

Groups larger than six tend to be unwieldy and have trouble finding enough camping space. But much of the success of the group depends on the kind of people in the group. No matter what size of group you hike with, you will likely learn many things about yourself.

Another thing you will likely learn is your physical capability. If you have never hiked before you could be pleasantly surprised by your stamina and inner courage. Or you could learn that your niche in life is behind a desk. But remember, the purpose of the hike is not to see how quickly you can reach the other end. If there are some members of your group who want to pretend that they are hares, let them go to the front of the hike. It happens over and over that the slow steady hikers are the ones who finish the trail in one piece and enjoy the whole trip. But there is also a limit to how slowly you should hike. If you dawdle you could end up camping under a tree with no fire and no dinner and get up in the morning with no sleep. And when you cross logs, your chances of falling increase with the time spent standing on them.

Of course some logs are so dangerous that they deserve absolute attention. In such cases a swig of booze is not appropriate, it dulls your senses, including balance. But booze can be useful. After a day's hiking a small drink can be a psychological boost, though alcohol is not a warming agent. Some hikers take along a mickey of rum, to sip from and make a small party out of. Once the liquor is finished it makes a good water bottle for the drier northern sections of the trail.

Crossing rivers is a special technique. If they are fast flowing, a stave is essential for maintaining balance. If there is a possibility of being swept away, ropes should be used and only one hiker sent at a time so that all of you don't get swept out to sea if one falls. If the river is rafted, the raft should be made out of large logs, more than 8" diameter and secured by several cross members. Nails can be scrounged from driftwood, or hikers can pack a few spikes with them. In either case, the nailed joints should be backed up by rope lashings (rope bends to take stress).

The raft can be sent across the river by dragging it upstream and having one person paddle like mad for the other side. He can secure a line to the other side of the creek and set up a return system. The first person to try the raft should do so without a pack in case the raft's engineering needs alterations before it is seaworthy. Once completed, rafts should be beached so that other groups can use them. Bits of rope, which can be usually found along the beaches, are good for mooring rafts.

As for wildlife, your chances of seeing eagles are excellent. There is a group living near Clo—oose, and another at the Walbran. Deer are seen occasionally but rarely bear. However bears have bothered people at some campsites in the Nitinat. As they are usually after food take the proper precaution and hang your food packs from a tree out of reach of any bear. Whether you take your dog on the trail, depends on the dog's size. Large dogs such as Alsatians and Labradors have difficulty going through thick brush and must be carried up the many ladders. Smaller dogs, however, have an easy time because they can go under the dense ground cover and are easily carried up ladders. Also small dogs eat less than large dogs.

The only other animals most hikers will encounter are mice or martens. They live on beaches and near the cabins and are particularly adept at gnawing through canvas so they can eat your bread. To guard against mice you can store your food in a plastic pack, or hang the food from a branch. Usually standing the pack against a wall or log and closing the flaps is sufficient to keep mice away.

And the last piece of advice is this: pack along an overdose of common sense, it could be the difference between a successful hike and a return trip to civilization via Air-Sea rescue. Most problems encountered on the hike can be surmounted by stopping to figure them out. As an example of what not to do, here is a true story of two hikers' misfortunes on the trail.

"We were a group of six that arrived in Clo—oose after some particularly rough hiking on the southern section. Four members of the group had to return to Vancouver in a few days so they stopped in Clo—oose only long enough to have lunch. The four then forged on, one up Nitinat Lake via boat and the other three to Bamfield by boat.

"The two who stayed in Clo—oose planned to stay there two nights and explore the area around the old village. On one day they explored a trail marked "Nitinat Narrows" and wound up in Whyac before returning to Clo—oose for the night. The next morning, when it was time to leave for Whyac, one of the hikers suggested they take a trail other than the one marked "Nitinat Narrows" since they had taken that one the previous day. He believed it was an alternate route to Whyac.

"Soon they realized the trail did not lead to Whyac since it ran in a generally north direction, so after a glimpse at their map they decided it must be an unmarked trail to a point just north of Whyac. When the trail finally came to an end it was at a small bay on Nitinat Lake and the two hikers guessed they were just around the corner from Whyac and could reach the village by going over a small hill that had been logged about eight years ago.

"After an hour of hiking through some of the thickest

scrub in B.C. the two hikers checked the map again and realized they had taken the trail to Brown's Bay and were thus more than a mile from Whyac. And they also realized they were hopelessly lost. They had no compass and the sun was useless for direction since it was obscured by clouds.

"By now it was late afternoon and the thought of reaching Whyac was abandoned. The ocean waves were barely audible and the foghorn off Clo—oose also could be heard. They decided to try for the ocean thinking they would soon meet the trail. With no compass the method of direction was to climb a hill, then climb a tree and try to see the ocean. About 6:30 p.m. (they had no watch) they realized they had no hope of getting out that day so they looked for a dry campsite. They found one where a tree had been uprooted many years ago. They made a good meal of their last egg and ham but had no water to drink since there were no streams nearby.

"It started to rain so they hung the plastic over the tent in such a manner as to collect rainwater for the morning. After a fair sleep and a hot porridge breakfast from the butane burner, the two hikers set out again in the general direction of the beach.

"Finally, the hiker more experienced with the coast (but an inexperienced hiker) persuaded the other to follow a stream in the hope that it would lead to the ocean, or if not the ocean, at least to Nitinat Lake.

"The hiking consisted of stumbling through salal, with head down and parting a path with gloved hands. Finally, the stream ran under a small bridge in the trail and they followed the trail into Clo—oose, but in the process they had crossed the trail without knowing it.

"That same day they arrived in Whyac and found the village deserted. So they settled down to a long stay and tried to catch a salmon that was jumping in the narrows."

But this story has a happy ending.

"We were just sitting in Whyac. I was drying out my clothes and the other hiker was trying to catch a fish when a float plane flew overhead. It came back, landed, and took us directly to Victoria harbour. It was looking for two other hikers who had made it out the night before."

Conservation

Vancouver Island is the first place in British Columbia where the myth of inexhaustible plenty is completely exposed and thus it is exceptionally important to secure adequate protection for recreation lands before it is too late.

To understand the issue let us go back to the 1950's when Justice Sloan chaired his two Royal Commissions of Enquiry into the Forest Industry. His main conclusion was that the Crown forests should be managed on a basis of sustained yield. To implement this the Forest Service, who were too short of funds and staff to administer all the lands directly, established many areas as Tree Farms which were then leased to various major companies. In this way virtually all the public forest land on Vancouver Island was committed to forestry with very minor attention being paid to the need for future recreation land. Essentially the present park system on the Island is what we will have in the year 2000 unless we can persuade the government to take some areas presently committed to forestry and turn them over to recreation.

In this regard the Nitinat Lakes and the West Coast Trail form an important precedent. The boundaries of the trail were provisionally set at a narrow strip half a mile wide except for enlargements at Cape Beale and Clo–oose, when the Pacific Rim National Park was created in 1969. The agreement between the federal and provincial authorities stated that the final boundaries were to be established before April 1974.

This is where the trouble starts, the tentative boundaries are inadequate to protect the character of the trail and have omitted

75

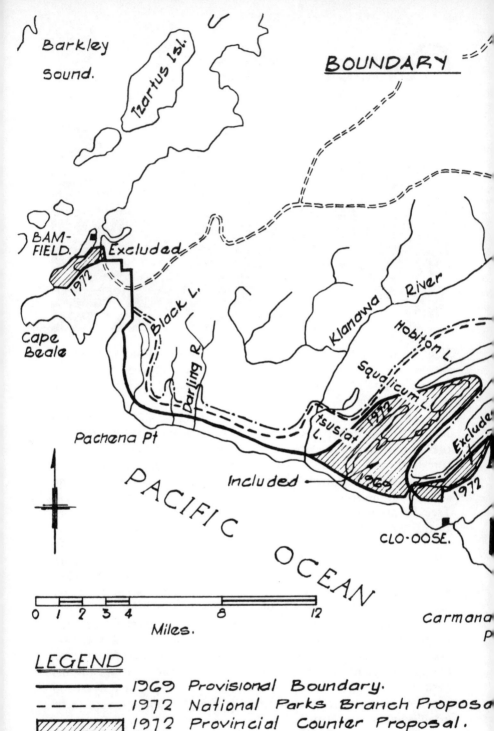

Barkley Sound.

Izartus Isl.

BOUNDARY

BAM-FIELD.

Excluded

1972

Cape Beale

Black L.

Darling R.

Klanawa River

Hobiton L.

Squalicum L.

Tsusiat L.

1972

Excluded

Pachena Pt

Included

1969

1972

CLO-OOSE.

PACIFIC OCEAN

0 1 2 3 4   8   12
Miles.

Carmana P

LEGEND

—————————— 1969 Provisional Boundary.

— — — — — 1972 National Parks Branch Proposa

▨▨▨▨▨ 1972 Provincial Counter Proposal.

—·—·—·—·— Sierra Club Proposal.

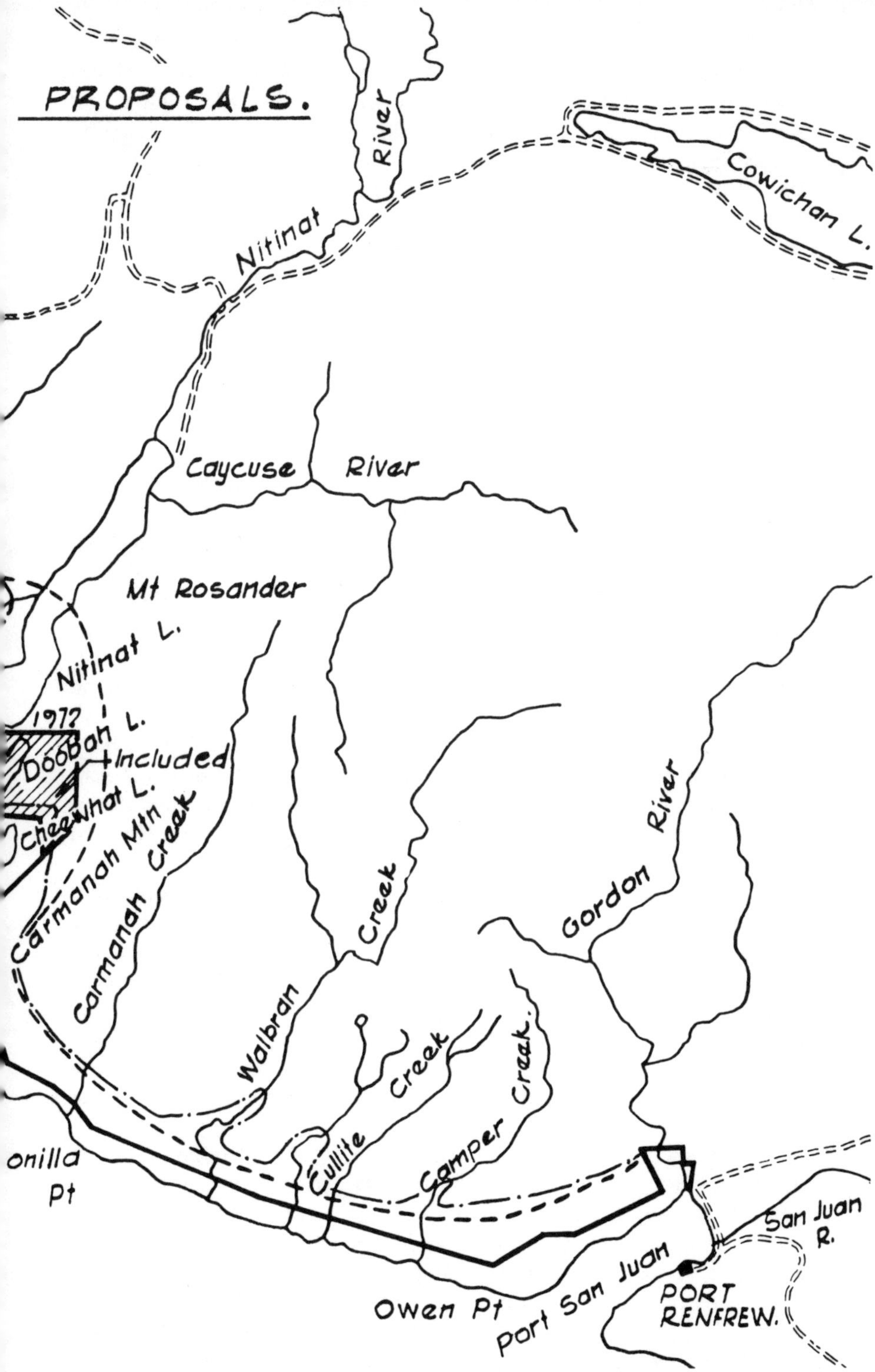

PROPOSALS.

River

Nitinat

Cowichan L.

Caycuse River

Mt Rosander

Nitinat L.

1972
DooBah L. ─Included
Cheewhat L.

Carmanah Mtn

Carmanah Creek

Gordon River

Creek

Walbran

Cullite Creek

Camper Creek

onilla
Pt

Owen Pt   Port San Juan

San Juan
R.

PORT
RENFREW.

the Nitinat Lakes, an area of exceptional recreation potential and scientific interest, and other attractive areas such as Black Lake and the lower reaches of the Klanawa. This mistake was recognized by the National Parks Branch in April 1970 when they approached the province with a request to include the Nitinat Lakes in the National Park. The province prodded by MacMillan Bloedel and B.C. Forest Products, the holders of the Tree Farm Licences 21 and 27 in the area, balked and that is when the argument started.

Let us examine first the need for wider boundaries for the West Coast Trail; at present the only land protected is the narrow coastal strip. When logging of the adjacent hinterland begins, logging roads will bring vehicle access to within half a mile of the coast almost along the total length of the trail. This half mile buffer is far too slim to prevent people pushing trails through from the logging roads to attractive spots such as Carmanah Beach, Tsusiat and the Klanawa. The result is easy to foresee, these areas will become heavily used and the trail will lose much of the natural and wild atmosphere which is its greatest charm. Instead of offering a chance for a long communication with things natural, the journey will be sadly cut up, a section of wild trail, an area of resident campers, established campsites and all the accoutrements of motorised camping. We will have allowed the rare and unusual to be reduced to the commonplace.

To prevent this type of intrusion the boundaries should have a minimum width of 1½ miles, that width of coastal scrub should be enough to deter most unauthorised trail makers. By comparison the Olympic Beach National Park in Washington State has an average width of over 2½ miles.

Such a width would also prevent much of the visual and noise impact of the adjacent logging operations on hikers. In particular it is important that the ocean face of Carmanah Mountain should not be logged because that face dominates many miles of the trail and the logging scars would spoil the natural scene of the trail.

The argument for inclusion of the Lower Klanawa, Black Lake and other attractive spots is to add variety for side trips from the main trail and for the provision of camp sites situated off the beach or main trail.

The arguments for the preservation of the Nitinat Lakes are different, though again are related to rarity of experience. Hobiton, Tsusiat and Squalicum Lakes offer safe canoe recreation which cannot be matched elsewhere on Vancouver Island. The lakes are at a low level, are warm and extremely beautiful.

However, their real impact is in their forest. When you move up the Hobiton River to Hobiton Lake and see the Hobiton-Tsusiat watershed open up in front of you, with the great sweep of forest rising from the lake up Hobiton Ridge you are looking at something very unusual, virtually the last low level accessible valley on Vancouver Island that is cloaked in its original virgin forest, and that has not been penetrated by man's economic activity.

To put this in perspective there are only two major portions of low level climax forest protected in British Columbia. The first is the Moyeha Valley in Strathcona Park and its protection is in doubt because Strathcona has only Class B status and can thus be logged. The second is the ecological reserve on East Redonda Island which is not open to the general public. The Moyeha is accessible only by boat or over a high mountain pass and is thus truly remote. The Nitinat forest is within 3 hours travel of Victoria yet the authorities seem blind to the significance of it.

To appreciate the impact of the Nitinat Forest it is important to appreciate its history and the changes that will be brought about by logging there. In the coastal zone the forest moves through several transitions before it reaches its climax state, which is defined as that state which reproduces itself. After a major fire or clearing the pioneer species are usually shrubs, weeds, and alder, these are followed by the Douglas Fir which cannot regenerate in shade and as the Douglas Fir ages and dies it is replaced by cedar-hemlock forest which regenerates itself, for the seedlings of these species can tolerate shade.

Thus the low level climax forest is a multi-age forest which may have taken up to 2000 years to evolve. It is characterized by having many enormous trees, many rotten, limited undergrowth making travel easy, but a forest floor rich with small plants, mosses, lichens and many curious items.

If this area is operated as a tree farm the present type of forest will be entirely eliminated, the old trees will be cut, the new forest will be planted with a Douglas Fir-hemlock mix, and will be cut after a period of about 80 years. Thus the replacement forest will have an entirely different character. For the first 20 years of the cycle the forest will be virtually impenetrable as the young growth rises, the richness of the forest floor will be gone, travel will be made much more difficult if we are to judge by the debris left in other logging operations, and the great trees will be gone.

We advertise British Columbia as the tourists' paradise and boast of how the tourist industry will soon overtake the forest industry as a dollar earner. Yet the government does not seem to have learned the obvious about the tourist: he does not travel to see what he can see at home, he travels to see the exceptional. The old climax forest of the Nitinat is exceptional, MacMillan Bloedel's uniform second growth is not. In the Nitinat and along the trail

Giant cedar, Hobiton forest.

Rafting Klanawa River.

the provincial authorities appear prepared to allow the exceptional to be eliminated without appreciating that it has special values. The parallel might be if the French were to strip Notre Dame Cathedral of all its treasures and advertise for tourists to come to view the shell.

But the Council of Forest Industries is lobbying the provincial government to prevent this precedent of land committed to forestry being removed for recreation, and they are being listened to. If the proposals of the National Parks Branch and conservationists were outrageous the CFI might have a point, but the proposals are modest and the CFI arguments are weak. As an example let us examine the effect of the loss to B.C. Forest Products of that portion of TFL 27 that lies in the Nitinat.

The Sierra Club has asked that 14,000 acres be withdrawn from TFL 27: this comprises the Hobiton, Tsusiat and Squalicum drainages, of which 4,000 acres are lake and some 2,000 acres around Tsusiat Lake are scrub and poor growth sites.

If we take the loss of productive forest area at 8,000 acres, then working on a sustained yield cycle of 80 years, the annual cut will be only about 100 acres. Yet BCFP has a total annual cut in the province of over 10,000 acres. Thus its annual yield from the proposed park extension would amount to about only 1% of its annual intake of timber.

It is fatuous to argue that such a small volume is essential to the operation of a major company which could obtain replacement timber by better utilisation of timber from its other holdings.

BCFP have stated that their major concern is to maintain employment at their Youbou Mill, but some of their staff tell us that only 15% of the timber supply for that mill comes from the Nitinat and that the mill will be closed in any event by 1982, for by then the company will have exhausted its other supplies of mature timber on Vancouver Island for which the mill is designed.

It is also interesting to note that BCFP and MB are two companies that have been criticised by the Minister of Forests for not adapting their mills fast enough to cope with the switch from old timber to second growth timber and by this omission, not utilising the young second growth thinnings on their tree farms. If these were used in special mills more employment would be created than would be lost by not logging the Nitinat. Unfortunately, our major forest companies appear to be committed to logging big trees.

It can be stated confidently that the loss of the Nitinat will create a minimum of difficulty for BCFP yet if added to the National Park system the forests of the Nitinat would be a real jewel. A similar analysis for the proposed extractions from TFL 21 would show they are not significant to the overall operation of MacMillan Bloedel.

There is a scientific gain to the inclusion of the Nitinat forest in the National Park. As yet we have preserved no complete drainage basins in their natural state. We have accepted the word of the foresters that they can maintain a sustained harvest from our forests. Yet we know that each cutting cycle is accompanied by erosion of soil and nutrients.

To check on the foresters' claims some watersheds should be retained in an untouched state to be used as yardsticks against which the changes created by forestry can be assessed. If science, and recreation can be combined in this way, we would be very fortunate.

At present the proposals of the National Parks Branch and the Sierra Club have been endorsed by every major conservation group in British Columbia, detailed submissions and appeals have been made to the provincial cabinet and its Environment and Land Use Committee. The only response of the provincial government has been an offer to adjust the boundaries to include 8,000 acres of the Nitinat Lakes, excluding all the Hobiton drainage, and the logged off area around Sprise Lake. In return they have asked for land at Brady Beach on Cape Beale, and around Brown's Bay to be excluded from the Park, and in addition have requested that the National Parks Branch exchange the 8,000 acres in the Nitinat for 8,000 acres of land presently included in the Long Beach section of the National Park but lying east of the Tofino-Ucluelet highway.

This proposal is completely unacceptable. No extra protection is offered for the West Coast Trail, the precedent of land exchanges involving committed park land should not be set, and the best part of the Nitinat Lakes, Hobiton Lake has been omitted. The proposal neatly severs the old and majestic timber of Hobiton from the old but scrubby timber of Tsusiat. The desire of the province to regain control of land near Long Beach, at Brady Beach and Brown's Bay, scares many observers. We are forced to ask why these lands are wanted: there is already talk of a proposal for a large scale marina development at Brown's Bay. Such commercial schemes adjacent to the National Parks may be highly profitable, but might in turn do much to harm the Park.

The Sierra Club believes that both provincial and federal agencies must be made aware of the popular feeling that more recreation land is needed, and the general disatisfaction with the multiple use philosophy pushed by the Forest Service and the forest industry. If this is a viable philosophy then it should be tested in areas that have been penetrated already and not in our last and most valuable wild areas. The valley of Nitinat Lake

82

obviously should be managed in this way as a buffer between the wild coast and the logging of the interior of the Island.

A minor victory has been won in the Hobiton area, for after protests the logging road into Hobiton Lake has been halted, but construction could be restarted at any time. MacMillan Bloedel are initiating new logging near Black Lake, the Lower Klanawa and the north side of the Gordon River, all of which are critical areas.

The provincial authorities can be induced to negotiate a reasonable solution only through public pressure. If you have enjoyed the West Coast Trail or the Lakes of the Nitinat, the Sierra Club urges you to assist their preservation by writing to those in control stating your views.

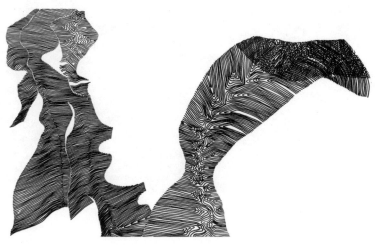

Trail near Pachena.

Action Line

This book has been published to encourage you to visit the West Coast Trail and the Nitinat to see for yourself what the community is about to lose. We are confident that having seen these areas, you will want to play a part in conserving them for the enjoyment of future generations.

The most effective way of helping is to write to the men whose decisions control the Nitinat and the Trail; they are Premier Bennett, the Hon. Ray Williston, and the Hon. Jean Chretien. Write to them and tell them of your appreciation of the area and request that all the Hobiton-Tsusiat valley be included in the National Park, and that the West Coast Trail be given adequate protection by increasing the width of its protective strip to at least 1½ miles.

Their addresses are as follows:

> Premier W.A.C. Bennett
> Parliament Buildings
> Victoria, B.C.

> Hon. Ray Williston
> Minister for Lands and Forests
> Parliament Buildings
> Victoria, B.C.

> Hon. Jean Chretien
> Minister for Indian Affairs and Northern Development
> Parliament Buildings
> Ottawa, Ont.

Should you require further information or wish to pass on exploration knowledge, or to contribute to or work for the cause, please contact:

Sierra Club of B.C.　　　　　or　　　　　Sierra Club of B.C.
1572 Monterey Avenue　　　　　　　　　　Box 385
Victoria, B.C.　　　　　　　　　　　　　　West Vancouver, B.C.
Area Code 604
598-5524 or 477-2687